THE FISHER KING

The Book of the Film

Other Titles from the Applause Screenplay Series

THE ADVENTURES OF BARON MUNCHAUSEN
Charles McKeown and Terry Gilliam

ERIK THE VIKING
Terry Jones

A FISH CALLED WANDA
John Cleese and Charles Crichton

JACOB'S LADDER
Bruce Joel Rubin

TERMINATOR 2: JUDGMENT DAY
The Book of the Film: An Illustrated Screenplay
James Cameron and William Wisher

THE FISHER KING

The Book of the Film

Richard LaGravanese
Introduction by Terry Gilliam

· Over 200 photographs ·
· A selection of deleted and altered scenes ·
· Original storyboards ·
· Interviews with Robin Williams and Terry Gilliam ·
· A symposium on the making of the film ·
· The complete credits ·

APPLAUSE
❦BOOKS❦

An Applause Original

THE FISHER KING
The Book of the Film

Copyright © 1991 Tri-Star Pictures Inc.

Interviews with Terry Gilliam and Robin Williams © 1990, 1991 by David Morgan.

Library of Congress Cataloging-in-Publication Data:

LaGravenese, Richard.
    The fisher king / Richard LaGravanese : introduction by Terry Gilliam.
        p.   cm. -- (The Applause screenplay series)
    "An Applause original."
    ISBN 1-55783-098-3 : $12.95
    I. Title. II. Series.
PN1997.F52 1991
791.43'72--dc20   91-31502
                                                       CIP

APPLAUSE THEATRE BOOK PUBLISHERS
211 West 71st Street
New York, NY 10023
Phone: 212-595-4735   Fax: 212-721-2856

First Applause Printing, 1991

"Printed by Data Reproduction Corporation, Rochester Hills, Michigan"

CONTENTS

INTRODUCTION

by Terry Gilliam

There it was. Lying on the kitchen counter. The "other" script. It was late ... sometime after one o'clock in the morning, I had finished reading the "important script ... the one that had been written and rewritten over the previous months ... the one that was going to be a major motion picture with incredible special effects, a huge budget and was a definite "green light." It was terrible and I felt resentful that I had wasted an evening reading it. All I wanted to do was to go to bed. But, as I passed the kitchen counter, the "other" script beckoned. My agent had sent it along with the "important" script, as an example of interesting writing. After what I had just read, I was slightly curious to find out what Hollywood considered to be interesting writing ... and so I opened it to the first page.

Two hours later, I finally put it down with one thought in mind: "Why didn't I write this?" Here were characters I understood fully, they were funny and moving and constantly surprising. Here were ideas and attitudes that were perfectly aligned to my own. Who was this Richard LaGravenese who had stolen my thoughts and then put them on paper far better than I could ever hope to do? How could this script have managed to run the gauntlet of studio executives and survive in such a quirky, original and virginal state? It certainly didn't read like a Hollywood script. I had a definite need to know more.

For years I had felt that the whole business of filmmaking was too hard and painful to expend time and energy on other people's ideas and, as a result, had always sworn I wouldn't do a film I hadn't initiated, that hadn't sprung from deep within the shallows of my own psyche, and yet, here I was, reading something with which I felt totally at ease. It was like a gift from cinema heaven, particularly in my post-*Munchausen* burned-out state ... feeling incapable, as I did, of ever tackling another gigantic project. In fact, I wasn't certain I could ever manage to make another film no matter what size ... and had been saying I would only try something very, very small — possibly a film about one person — a schizophrenic, but ... only half of his personality. I had also sworn, long ago, not to work in the States, especially directly for a Hollywood studio. "Well, ...," I though, "what are rules for — but to be broken? I made them ... I can break them." So I called my agent and told him that I was interested in finding out more about this "Fisher King" project.

It is now a year and half later. The film is done. I'm very proud to have been part of it. Most of the questions concerning the birth and childhood of the script have been answered. It has become increasingly clear that some sort of cinematic guardian angel has been hovering around this project from the beginning ... from the moment Richard, with no hope of it ever being produced, wrote the script for himself, as an exercise in screenplay writing. Through the dark days at Disney where they tried to turn it into a "caper" movie — complete with a Grail robbery on roller skates. To the risky choice of me as director. To the "greenlighting" of the project at a time when Tri-Star, the studio, was in complete flux. Right up to the moment the studio decided to release the picture in the autumn, rather than try to turn it into another *Pretty Woman* for summer, 1991.

Someone has been watching over *The Fisher King*.

We have been able to maintain a protective shell around the project that has allowed creativity to fumble around in the dark, making mistakes, finding confidence, and then, eventually, falling into happy, magical solutions. The piece has grown organically without interference from fearful executives. No chemical pesticides or artificial preservatives have been used. New ideas have come from so many sources that it becomes hard to remember who thought of what, but Jeff, Robin, Mercedes, and Amanda deserve enormous thanks for expanding what Richard had originally written. And Richard deserves even more for not being so protective of his work that all of us couldn't help contribute to making it blossom. To me the whole process has been one of total, open collaboration, but without a single Quisling in the lot.

Terry Gilliam

P.S. I told a lie ... there was one, but that's another story.

FADE IN:

1   INT.   **DARKENED BEDROOM — DAWN**

CLOSEUP ON RADIO/ALARM CLOCK reads 5:59 a.m. The digital
numbers flip to 6:00 and the radio goes on: a talk show host
speaks in a soft, soothing voice:

> JACK (V.O.)
> It's six a.m. ... Ooooooo and that bed
> never felt sooooo goooood ... Mmmm, you
> linger in a warm, gentle dream state ...
> ever so comfortable ... ever so safe ...

SFX: LOUD BATTLE NOISE

> JACK (V.O.)
> (continuing)
> ... *But suddenly you realize it's*
> *Monday!*

A woman SCREAMS ... the D.J., JACK, speaks at a rapid fire
pace ... a HAND from O.S. tries to shut the alarm off in the
dark.

> JACK (V.O.)
> (continuing)
> ... your hand races to shut off the
> alarm before your mind wakes up...

SCREAMS ... the HAND knocks over a water glass and grabs the
clock but can't find the off switch.

> JACK (V.O.)
> (continuing)
> ... But it's too late! If you don't get
> out of bed now, you'll never have enough
> time to blow dry your hair *that special*
> *way* ... You'll never make that nine
> o'clock meeting that your *partner will*
> *be early for* ... *You will be late and*
> *everyone will notice!*

The HAND bangs the clock violently ...

> JACK (V.O.)
> (continuing)
> ... Rumors will fly about you losing
> your edge ... Someone will casually
> mention they saw you downing shots of
> tequila at the Xmas party and before you
> know it, you're spilling your guts to a
> Senate committee or selling yourself on
> street corners to middle aged men from
> (MORE)

(CONTINUED)

1

1   CONTINUED:

JACK (V.O.) (CONTINUED)
the Midwest ... Headlines flash across
your mind — "*Sleeping Investment Banker
Guns D.J. Then Self — Claimed — 'I only
wanted two more minutes!'*"

SCREAMS ... SILENCE ... The D.J. (JACK) speaks in a normal
voice.

JACK (V.O.)
(continuing)
... Hey, it's Monday morning, and I'm
Jack Lucas.

The HAND rips the clock off the night table.

CUT TO:

2   **INT.   KITCHEN — MORNING**

A WOMAN in a bathrobe spoons the contents of a protein drink
called Executive Protein Blast into blender ...

WOMAN (V.O.)
(upset)
... I don't have to talk to you.

JACK (V.O.)
Yes ... Yes, you do because you see,
today, you're our ...

PRE-RECORDED ECHOING (V.O.)
Spotlight Celebrity.

CUT TO:

3   **INT.   BATHROOM — MORNING**

A naked MAN shaves as he listens to the radio.

JACK (V.O.)
And in the spirit of fairness, we want
the public to hear your side of things.
So now ... how long were you and Senator
Payton having this sleazy affair?

WOMAN (V.O.)
(angry)
I am tired of the public thinking
they've got the right to invade a
person's private life.

2

4   INT.   BATHROOM — MORNING

A WOMAN sensually applying lipstick and makeup as:

                    JACK (V.O.)
          Oh please! ... You had sex with a United
          States Senator in the parking lot of Sea
          World ... You're telling me you're a
          private kind of person. No ... you're
          our ...

                    PRE-RECORDED ECHOING (V.O.)
          Spotlight Celebrity ...

                    WOMAN (V.O.)
          That's still all anybody talks about.
          Nobody even thinks to ask whether we
          loved each other.

4A   EXT.   WALL STREET AREA — MORNING

Hordes of BUSINESS PEOPLE stampeding towards their jobs ...

                    JACK (V.O.)
          Because nobody cares about that, sweet-
          heart. Nobody wants to hear about your
          romantic love. No. We want to hear about
          the back seats of limos ... the ruined
          lives of people we want to be ... new
          and exotic uses for champagne corks ...

5   INT.   COFFEE SHOP — MORNING

PEOPLE line up to buy coffee and danish.

                    WOMAN (V.O.)
          Listen, I have been humiliated enough
          already!

                    JACK (V.O.)
          Perhaps not — We need those details ...

The WOMAN hangs up ...

                    JACK AND CREW
          Ooooo ...

                                             CUT TO:

5B   INT.   GRAND CENTRAL STATION — MORNING

Escalators packed with PEOPLE move like conveyor belts:

                                          (CONTINUED)

3

> JACK (V.O.)
> Hi, this is Jack Lucas and we're
> discussing personal pet peeves. Go
> ahead, caller.

> CALLER (V.O.)
> Okay ... well ... it's my husband ...

> JACK (V.O.)
> Huh-huh.

5C   INT.   **GRAND CENTRAL — MAIN FLOOR — MORNING**

Hundreds of PEOPLE moving like ants in every direction:

> CALLER (V.O.)
> He drives me crazy. I'll be talking and
> he'll never let me finish a sentence ...
> He's always finishing my ...

> JACK (V.O.)
> (overlaps)
> — Finishing your thoughts. That's awful.

5D   EXT.   **MIDTOWN NEW YORK — MORNING**

Midtown traffic. Angry CAB DRIVERS yelling at PEDESTRIANS.

> CALLER (V.O.)
> Oh! It absolutely drives me ...

> JACK (V.O.)
> (cuts her off)
> — Drives you crazy, huh? The scoundrel.

CUT TO:

5E   EXT.   **30 ROCKEFELLER PLAZA — MORNING**

> CALLER (V.O.)
> Hello Jack. It's Edwin.

> JACK AND CREW (V.O.)
> *It's Edwin!!!!*

"HAPPY DAYS ARE HERE AGAIN" plays then is abruptly stopped.

> JACK (V.O.)
> (continuing)
> Edwin. We haven't heard from you in what
> — a day? ... I've missed you.

5F   INT.   EDWIN'S APARTMENT — MORNING

INTERCUT EDWIN on phone.

6   INT.   RADIO STATION — MORNING

OVERHEAD SHOT of RADIO HOST as he speaks, while he
manipulates tapes, dials, switches, etc. ... at a breakneck
speed ...

                    EDWIN (V.O.)
            I've missed you too, Jack.

                    JACK AND CREW (O.S.)
            Awwww.....!

SFX: "A SUMMER PLACE" — THE NEEDLE IS SCRATCHED OFF

EDWIN laughs, perhaps a bit over zealously — He is a simple-
minded soul ... a lonely child in the body of a lonely man.

                    JACK (O.S.)
            So, Edwin baby, this is Sunrise
            Confession time ... what have you got
            for us?

                    EDWIN (V.O.)
            I ... I ... went to this bar ... this
            very, ya know — hard-to-get-in place ...
            called Babbitt's ...

The hands of the RADIO HOST pushing buttons, bending a
paperclip out of shape ...

                    JACK (O.S.)
            Yeah, I know the place. It's one of
            those chic *yuppie* gathering holes.

                    EDWIN (V.O.)
                (simple minded laughter)
            Okay ... I know but ... I met this
            beautiful girl ...

HOST's HANDS pop in a tape: "WEDDING BELLS," then a NEEDLE
scratching it off.

                    JACK (O.S.)
            Now, Edwin, if you start telling me
            you're in love again, I'm going to have
            to remind you of the time we made you
            propose to that check-out girl at
            Thrifty's that you liked so much.
            Remember her reaction ...

                                        (CONTINUED)

5

Another TAPE, another button pressed:

> BLACK SEVENTIES GROUP (V.O.)
> (sings)
> "Mister Big Stuff ... Huh ... Tell me
> ... Who do you think you are ... Mister
> Big Stuff ... you're never gonna get my
> love ..."

> EDWIN (V.O.)
> (defensive)
> I wasn't serious about her, Jack. That
> was just a joke for you guys ... She was
> just a girl. This is a beautiful woman.
> She wears pearls.

CAMERA KEEPS MOVING about the studio and the HOST, but we
never see his face:

> JACK (O.S.)
> Yeah, but does she swallow, Edwin?

> EDWIN (V.O.)
> I think she likes me ... she gave me her
> number, but she must work a lot cause when
> I call she's never home ... But I think
> we'll go out this weekend ... I've ...

> JACK (O.S.)
> Yeah, Edwin, *sure* ... and *Pinnochio* is a
> true story ... *Edwin! Wake up!* This is a
> fairytale ...

The CREW perform their duties with little enthusiasm.

> EDWIN (V.O.)
> No, Jack, no it's not ... She likes me.

> JACK (O.S.)
> She gave you the old brusheroo, kiddo
> ... Believe me — this tart will never
> make it to your dessert plate ...

> EDWIN (V.O.)
> (hurt)
> She *likes* me. She said for me to call!

> MICHAEL McDONALD (V.O.)
> (sings)
> "What a fool believes ... He sees ..."

> EDWIN (V.O.)
> (over the song)
> *Jack!*

(CONTINUED)

> JACK (O.S.)
> Edwin ... Edwin ... Edwin ... I told you
> about these people. They only mate with
> their own kind. It's called *Yuppie-In-*
> *Breeding* ... that's why so many of them
> are retarded and wear the same clothes.
> They're not human. They can't feel love.
> They can only negotiate love moments.
> They're evil, Edwin. They're repulsed by
> imperfection and horrified by the banal
> — everything America stands for. Edwin,
> they have to be stopped before it's too
> late. It's us or them.

Slight pause as EDWIN considers this.

> EDWIN (V.O.)
> (serious)
> Okay, Jack.

END CREDITS.

CAMERA PANS from a wall clock as JACK LUCAS winds up his
broadcast:

> JACK (O.S.)
> Well, folks ... It's been a thrill, as
> always.
> (false sincerity)
> "Have a perfect day" ...

We PAN several STUDIO TECHNICIANS making ready for the end
of the broadcast to the talk show host JACK LUCAS —
handsome, aggressive, intelligent — an underground media
star.

> JACK
> Everyone here on the Jack Lucas Morning
> Show says "bye".

> CREW
> *Bye!*

> JACK

> This is Jack Lucas ... So long ...
> arriverderch ... I'll be sure to send
> you a thought as I lie in the backseat
> of my stretch limo, have sex with the
> teenager of my choice ... And that
> thought will be: Thank God I'm me!

JACK motions to a TECHY behind glass. Then leans back in his
chair, as a RADIO COMMERCIAL begins.

His expression seems grave — not one you would expect after

(CONTINUED)

a successful broadcast. He appears tired and annoyed. He
sighs in relief that it is over. The STUDIO TEAM work around
him in silence — with no indication of the relationship they
have "on air." JACK pulls out a bottle of aspirins and takes
two.

>   JACK
>   (continuing; annoyed, to the
>   room)
>   I want you all to know I'mm getting sick
>   again and it's because someone keeps
>   forgetting to raise the thermostat
>   before I come in here ... My fucking ass
>   is freezing for the first hour.

A TECHY makes mocking faces behind his back. Another TECHY
suppresses a laugh.

>   CUT TO:

6A   EXT.   STREET/INT. LIMOUSINE — DAY

CLOSEUP of a script entitled: "On The Radio," a situation
comedy by Alan Siegal.

LOU ROSEN, JACK's agent, who sits in the back seat beside
JACK, thumbing through the script and chuckling to himself.
JACK stares in silence out the window.

>   LOU
>   You know some of this is very funny.
>   Cheever told me they've even secured the
>   rights to the Donna Summer song to play
>   over the credits.

>   JACK
>   (deadpan indifference)
>   Ooooo, I have chills ...
>   (deadpan interest)
>   Are you sure they want me? I won't read
>   unless I have an offer.

>   LOU
>   Jack, of course ... Not even a question.
>   When I spoke to him on the phone this
>   morning, I could actually smell how much
>   they want you for it. I could smell it
>   over the phone.

A STREET BUM, half dressed, walks in between the stopped
cars, banging on the windows and asking for money. He bangs
on JACK's window. JACK stares at him through the tinted
glass.

>   (CONTINUED)

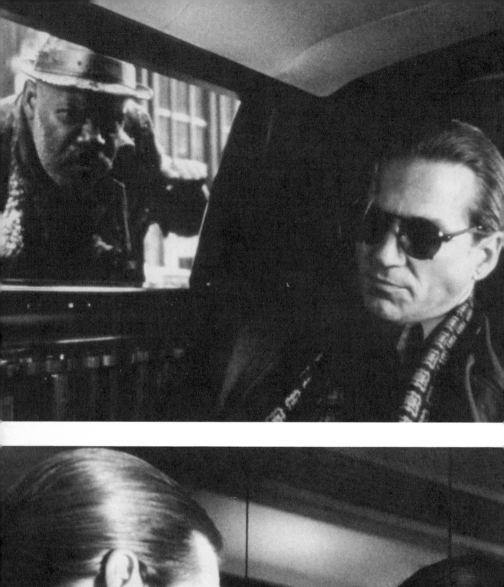

>   LOU
>   (continuing; looking through his
>   pockets)
> I don't think I have any change.

>   JACK
>   (adamant)
> I am not opening this window.
>   (looks at the BUM)
> A couple of quarters isn't going to make
> any difference anyway.

The BUM looks at the reflection of himself in the mirrored
window.

                                            CUT TO:

7   INT.   JACK'S APARTMENT — DAY

An expansive Tribeca loft. The modern, minimalist decor
gives it a sleek, cold feeling. A space full of glass,
angles and edges, with no place to feel safe and sound.

                                            CUT TO:

8   INT.   JACK'S APARTMENT — KITCHEN — DAY

The mirrored door closes revealing JACK's reflection — He
takes a good look at his face in the mirror — admiring every
contour, every pore. He mumbles as he's making coffee.

>   JACK
> I hate my cheeks.

                                            CUT TO:

9   INT.   JACK'S APARTMENT — DAY

JACK's girlfriend SONDRA — an artist with a beautifully
sculptured face and body — sleek, cold; like JACK's
apartment, she is eating a bowl of cereal, studying the
cereal box. Beside her is a sketchpad with an ink drawing of
a stalk of wheat (similar to the cereal box) growing out of
the belly button of a naked male figure whose torso/pelvis
is shaped like a map of America. JACK enters, toweling his
hair.

>   JACK
> Can I ask that when you clean your hands
> you wipe the ink off the inside of the
> sink before it stains the stainless
> steel?

>   SONDRA
>   (without looking up)
> You can ask.

JACK exits.

10   INT.   JACK'S APARTMENT — DAY

JACK has in his hand the television script entitled "On the Radio."

>   SONDRA (O.S.)
>   Raoul called before. About dinner.

JACK quickly opens his eyes. SONDRA crosses to the wall of closets and begins to undress.

>   JACK
>   About dinner as a concept or about
>   dinner with ...
>   (over-enunciating)
>   *Raoul?*

>   SONDRA
>   (deadpan)
>   You're so witty. I'm so jealous ... I
>   NEED to get out of here, Jack, and do
>   something other than sit in this apart-
>   ment and count how many funny lines you
>   have per page.

>   JACK
>   You know, tommorrow's a very big day for
>   me ... It would be nice if you pretended
>   like you understood.

>   SONDRA
>   Fine. I'll say no.

>   JACK
>   They're putting me on film tomorrow.

>   SONDRA (O.S.)
>   (peeved)
>   Fine.

>   JACK
>   (deeply felt)
>   ... First time in my life I'll be a
>   voice with a body. Do you know what that
>   means? What this could lead to?

>   SONDRA
>   (unsnapping her bra in the
>   front)
>   It's a sitcom, Jack — you're not
>   defining Pi.

>   JACK
>   I'll remember that the next time you get
>   (MORE)

(CONTINUED)

                              JACK (CONTINUED)
          excited by drawing pubic hairs on Raisin
          Bran ...
                    (lighting a joint and inhaling)
          Want some?

                              SONDRA
          No, I have to work.

                              JACK
          How un-sixties of you.

                              SONDRA
          I was nine in the sixties.

                              JACK
          I used to think my biography would be
          JACK LUCAS — THE FACE BEHIND THE VOICE,
          but now it can be JACK LUCAS THE FACE
          "AND" THE VOICE ... or maybe just JACK —
          EXCLAMATION POINT ...

10   PT   JACK'S POV —

SONDRA slips off her top as she climbs the stairs. JACK eyes
her sexy back. Feeling sexy, he rises and follows her.

11   INT.   BATHROOM — NIGHT

SONDRA leans over and turns on the shower.

JACK's naked legs enter the bathroom behind her and he
closes the door. CAMERA ON BATHROOM DOOR as we hear:

                              SONDRA (O.S.)
                    (annoyed)
          Jack, I have work to do, too.

JACK seduces SONDRA O.S.

                              SONDRA (O.S.)
          ... Can't we do this later? ...
                    (pause)
          All right ... well ... If we do this
          now, can I have dinner with Raoul?

                                                       CUT TO:

12C   INT.   BATHROOM FLOOR

CAMERA PANS a brown paper bag, a plate of half-eaten Chinese
food, a bottle of beer into a bathtub where JACK languishes

                                              (CONTINUED)

in a bubble bath studying his script. In the B.G. we hear Ella
Fitzgerald singing, "I've Got The World On A String" ...

> JACK
> "Hey ... for- ..."

False start. JACK clears his throat, pauses, then tries
again ...

>> (sarcastic ... insincere ...)
> "Hey! Forgiiiive ME!"

CUT TO:

13   INT.   JACK'S APARTMENT — NIGHT

Alarm clock reads 11:15. JACK is still rehearsing, while the
TV plays with no sound.

> JACK
> "HEY! Forgive MEEE!" ...
> FOR-GIVE-ME ...
> Hey ... forgive me!
>> (he smiles and shuts the script)
> ... I have this ... I really have this ...

He tosses the script aside and rubs his head. He suddenly
notices, on the soundless TV, a picture of himself on a news
broadcast. Confused, he raises the volume with the remote.

CUT TO:

13A   INT.   TV STATION — NEWS DESK — NIGHT

A news broadcast: a REPORTER in mid-report.

> JACK'S VOICE OVER
> "... everything America stands for.
> Edwin, they have to be stopped before
> it's too late ... It's us or them."

> REPORTER
> It was Mr. Lucas's off-handed remark
> that seemed to have a fatal impact on
> Mr. Malnick ...

CUT TO:

13B   EXT.   BABBITT'S — NIGHT

> REPORTER (V.O.)
> An after work night spot, Babbitt's is
> popular with single young professionals.

(CONTINUED)

                         REPORTER ON SCENE
              Edwin Malnick arrived at the peak hour
              of seven-fifteen, took one long look at
              the handsome collection of the city's
              best and brightest — then removed a shot-
              gun from his overcoat and opened fire.

JACK's face turns white.

                                                    CUT TO:

13C   INT.   **BABBITT'S — NIGHT**

To be INTERCUT with JACK's apartment.

The bar's glass has been blasted. Tables are overturned.
PARAMEDICS are running about.

                         REPORTER
              Seven people were killed before Mr.
              Malnick ...

A PICTURE OF EDWIN MALNICK is shown as the REPORTER
continues:

                         REPORTER
                      (continuing)
              ... turned the gun on himself and shot a
              hole through his head ...

EDWIN MALNICK looked sad and harmless. JACK quickly grabs
the phone and re-plugs it. He is about to make a call when
he is stopped by the REPORTER mentioning his name ...

                         REPORTER
                      (continuing)
              ... Representatives of radio cult
              personality Jack Lucas expressed regret,
              however no formal comment has been made.
              None of Babbitt's regulars had ever seen
              Edwin Malnick before ... but tonight,
              few will soon forget this lonely man —
              who reached out to a world he knew only
              through the radio — looking for friend-
              ship ... and finding only pain ... and
              tragedy ... This is Mark Saffron ...
              Channel Ten News.

JACK is frozen. His breathing grows heavy. His phone begins
to ring. But JACK is unable to move.

                                                    CUT TO:

14   EXT.   **VIDEO SPOT — DAY**

CAMERA PANS DOWN from the tall skyscrapers to the tiny video
store that sits as if in a valley between two mountains. PAN

                                                (CONTINUED)

14   CONTINUED:

toward the store as we follow a CUSTOMER through the door we
SUPERIMPOSE: A YEAR OR SO LATER.

CUT TO:

15   INT.   VIDEO SPOT — DAY

CAMERA TRACKS through a variety of CUSTOMERS looking through
the rentals, past the counter where EMPLOYEES are helping
the clientele and into the:

16   INT.   VIDEO SPOT OFFICE

Continuing to a CLOSEUP of the headline of a sensationalist
tabloid — "WOMAN KILLS PLASTIC SURGEON THEN SELF, TOLD
FRIENDS; I CAN'T BLINK WITHOUT PAIN."

The picture of a bug-eyed society woman is below the
caption. A HAND comes out from behind the paper, reaching
for a bottle of scotch on the table. The bottle disappears
behind the paper.

ANNE, the owner of the store, enters abruptly — closing the
office door behind her, a cigarette dangling from her mouth.
Her desk is organized litter — her walls are filled with
porno tapes. She searches for one as she talks:

> ANNE:
> These people are insane today. They took
> insane pills ...

A bit about ANNE as she searches for a video: ANNE is in her
mid-to-late thirties ... and she is all woman! She has a
raw, earthy, unmistakable sensuality. Her red lipstick
matches her red nail polish like a hat and glove set. Inlaid
on each nail is a rhinestone design of a little star. Her
angora sweaters are tight and clinging, giving her breasts a
decided lift and perkiness. Her backless pumps slap the
ground. A half-smoked cigarette hangs out of her mouth with
great expertise — a skill ANNE obviously picked up in a high
school bathroom. Her voice is thick with a delicious
Brooklyn twang. She is pure streetwise in attitude, philosophy and emotions. She turns and speaks to the MAN behind the
tabloid.

> ANNE
> (continuing)
> Hey! Mr. Happiness!

The MAN lowers the newspaper: it is JACK LUCAS; no longer
the aggressive radio star but more — a man who looks like he
hasn't slept in months. An intolerant, paranoid, self-
pitying misanthrope. The outrageous articles fascinate him.
ANNE removes the paper and scotch bottle.

(CONTINUED)

14

>   ANNE
>   (continuing)
>   Are we going to work today or what?

JACK stares back. ANNE waits for an answer. JACK looks
through the open office door and sees the store is packed
with rush hour CUSTOMERS — any one, a potential mass
murderer.

>   ANNE
>   (continuing)
>   *Hello!!!*

JACK jumps a bit then rises and crosses out the door
cautiously.

>   CUT TO:

17   **INT. VIDEO SPOT — DAY**

JACK's POV — CAMERA moves "cautiously," taking in the crowd
as they move about the walls of movies. Suddenly, the giant
face of a FRUMPY SECRETARY — POPS INTO FRAME.

>   FRUMPY SECRETARY
>   Can you help me! ...

JACK subtly shudders at the surprise. He stares deadpan.

>   FRUMPY SECRETARY
>   (continuing)
>   ... I'm at an absolute loss. I've been
>   looking for an hour — I'm losing my
>   mind.
>   (overly dramatic, rambling on)
>   ... I'm sort of in the mood for a
>   Katharine Hepburny, Cary Granty kinda
>   thing — Nothing heavy ... I couldn't
>   take heavy. Somethin' zany. I need zany.

JACK stares at her, at a loss. She gets an inspiration.

>   FRUMPY SECRETARY
>   ... OH! OH! Do you have anything with
>   that ... comedian who's on that show?
>   What's it — "On That Radio!" Ya know,
>   the guy that says "HEY ... FORGIVE ME
>   ...!"

JACK grinds his teeth and stares like a madman while ANNE,
aware of the effect this phrase has on him, throws a worried
look from the cash register. The FRUMPY SECRETARY laughs:

>   FRUMPY SECRETARY
>   I get such a kick outta the way he says
>   that ... He's so adorable! Didn't he
>   (MORE)

>   (CONTINUED)

>   FRUMPY SECRETARY (CONTINUED)
>   make a movie? ... I need something like
>   that — a funny, no brainy kinda thing.

JACK stares at the WOMAN manically then turns to the shelves
of movies behind the desk. Selecting one, he hands it to
her.

>   FRUMPY SECRETARY
>   Great ...
>   (reading box aloud)
>   "ORDINARY PEEPHOLES"

The WOMAN's eyes go wide. JACK stares at her deadpan.

>   JACK
>   It's kind of a — Big Titty-Spread Cheeky
>   kinda thing ...

ANNE, who has heard this entire exchange, has to bite her
lip to prevent herself from laughing ... She pulls JACK
away.

>   ANNE
>   ... I'm sorry.
>   (almost laughing)
>   I need to borrow him for a moment.

As ANNE tugs at his sleeve, JACK eyes the WOMAN like a
maniac being led away from his prey.

18   INT.   VIDEO SPOT OFFICE — DAY

ANNE stands before JACK who leans against her office door.

>   ANNE
>   Are you in a mood today baby? Is this
>   one of those days when you're in ...
>   whaddaya call it ... an emotional abyss?
>   Talk to me, cause I don't understand
>   these moods.

>   JACK
>   Anne, they're MY moods. If you want to
>   understand moods, have one of your own!

>   ANNE
>   Why don't you go upstairs ... take the
>   day off. All right? ... I'll cook
>   tonight.

She kisses him, then exits. JACK is not comforted in the
least by this show of affection — especially when he notices
her bra strap sticking out from her sweater.

>   (CONTINUED)

                        JACK
            Are you going for a specific look with
            this?

                                          CUT TO:

18A INT.   ANNE'S APARTMENT ABOVE VIDEO SPOT — NIGHT (RAINING)

ANNE and JACK sit around a formica kitchen table in silence
after eating dinner. ANNE smokes a cigarette. A portable TV
sits on a stand before them —

18AB SITCOM ON TV (INTERCUT WITH ANNE'S APARTMENT)

We hear a STUDIO AUDIENCE laughing on the TV ... ANNE
herself can't help but laugh. She snorts from trying to keep
it in. JACK shoots her a dirty look.

                        ANNE
            Well, it's funny! Whaddaya want from me?

                        JACK
            It's not funny. It's ... sophomoric and
            mindless ... and dumb.

                        ANNE
            Then why the hell do we watch it all the
            time?

                        JACK
                (in one breath)
            Because it makes me feel good to see how
            not funny it is and how America doesn't
            know the first thing about funny which
            makes it easier not being a famous funny
            TV celebrity because that would mean
            that I'm not really talented.

                        TV ACTOR (V.O.)
            Well forgiivvee meee ...

APPLAUSE and LAUGHTER ... ANNE just stares at JACK.

                        ANNE
            You're a sick fuck ... I don't know why
            you torture yourself.
                (she hits his head)
            Too many thoughts — too crowded in
            there. You should read a book.

She picks up her paperback and begins to read.

                        JACK
            It's important to think. It's what
            separates us from lentils ... and people
                (MORE)

                                       (CONTINUED)

                         JACK (CONTINUED)
          who read books like ...
                    (reading her paperback cover)
          ... "Love's Flower Bed."

He gets up to get a drink from ANNE's makeshift bar.

                         ANNE
                    (defensive)
          It happens to be a beautiful love story.
                    (hurt)
          Ya know, you used to like that about me.
          You used to say you liked that I didn't
          make you think so much. That we could be
          together and not think ...

                         JACK
          Yeah, well ... suicidal paranoiacs say
          funny things sometimes.

ANNE is deeply hurt by this. She gathers her dignity and
exits into the bedroom, slamming the door behind her. JACK
downs his drink as the sitcom returns to the TV O.S.

                         TV ACTOR (V.O.)
          *I hope when I'm your age you're finally
          dead!*

Big laughter.

                         JACK
          Madness.

Fed up, JACK throws his coat on, storms out and slams the
door.

                                             CUT TO:

18B   EXT.   VIDEO POP — NIGHT (RAINY)

JACK exits into the rain, tearing his coat on the front
door.

                                             CUT TO:

18C   EXT.   STREET — NIGHT

JACK, depressed and wet, walks the streets of New York.

                                             CUT TO:

18D   EXT.   JACK'S OLD APARTMENT BUILDING — NIGHT

JACK stands before his old building, looking at it
longingly.

19   EXT.   PLAZA HOTEL — NIGHT — RAIN

A wet JACK stops to watch the goings on at the entrance. He
sees a limousine at the Plaza — parked and awaiting its
occupants. A handsome MAN in his forties exits the hotel and
walks toward the limo. He is holding the hand of his six-
year-old SON, who is carrying a two foot high plastic,
smiling Pinnochio doll. Both FATHER and SON are dressed in
ties and jackets. JACK watches in envy. His ripped, wet
clothes are a shabby reflection of the MAN's. He eyes the
limo with longing. As the MAN tips the doorman, a BUM
approaches and asks for money. When the MAN refuses and
turns his back to enter the limo, the BUM becomes aggressive
and starts pulling at the MAN's jacket and yells:

> BUM
> *Merry fucking Christmas ... Happy*
> *fucking New Year!!*

He continues to harrass the MAN, who pushes his SON away.
The DOORMAN comes to the MAN's rescue. As they BOTH try to
pull the BUM off the MAN, the six-year-old SON notices JACK
and walks calmly over.

JACK, mesmerized by the scene, doesn't notice the BOY.

> BOY (O.S.)
> Mr. Bum

JACK looks down. The BOY stands directly before him. JACK
sort of smiles. The BOY extends his arms a offers the
Pinnochio doll to JACK. JACK is confused but the BOY simply
deposits the doll into his arms and walks back to the limo.
By that time, the BUM is being held by the DOORMAN, and both
FATHER and SON enter the limo.

JACK holds the doll. He is surrounded by STREET PEOPLE
asleep or drunk on the sidewalk near the hotel. He angrily
realizes there's not much difference between him and them.

> JACK
> Anybody here named Jimeny!

A DRUNK groans. JACK snaps the doll under his arm and walks
O.S.

CUT TO:

20   STATUE NEAR PLAZA — RAIN

TIGHT SHOT of newspaper front page on sidewalk ... Headline
reads: "FIFTH HOMELESS MAN FOUND BURNED ALIVE" ... CAMERA
MOVES OUT to reveal that the paper is covering the head of a
STREET PERSON sleeping on the edge of the stone, flowered

(CONTINUED)

dividers on Park Ave. ... CAMERA pans over to a drunken JACK, sitting on the sidewalk against the divider, having a conversation with Pinnochio beside him.

> JACK
> You ever read any Nietzsche? ...

The similing Pinnochio clearly has not.

> JACK
> (continuing)
> Nietzche says that there are two kinds of people in this world ... People who are destined for greatness like ... Walt Disney and ... Hitler ... and then there's the rest of us ... He called us the Bungled and Botched. We get teased. We sometimes get close to greatness but we never get there. We're the expendable masses. We get pushed in front of trains ... take poison aspirins ... get gunned down in Dairy Queens ...

He drinks from his Jack Daniels bottle ...

> JACK
> (continuing)
> You wanna hear my new title for my biography, my little Italian friend ... "It Was No Fucking Picnic — The Jack Lucas Story." Like it? ... Just nod yes or no ...
> (tries it in Pig-Italian)
> "Il Nouva Esta Fuckin' Pinicko" —
> (he smiles)
> You're a good kid ... Just say no to drugs ...
> (he nods and drinks)
> Ya ever get the feeling sometimes ... you're being punished for your sins ...?

                                                    CUT TO:

21   EXT.   EAST RIVER, NEW YORK CITY — NIGHT

CLOSEUP of two feet standing beneath the railing overlooking the East River. Taped to one ankle is a brick. Taped to the other is a smiling Pinnochio doll. An empty bottle of liquor drops to the ground and SHATTERS.

JACK stands prepared to surrender his fate and make the final leap. He stares at the river, almost smiling. He has made his decision. He is calm and serene. He raises his foot over the railing.

                                                (CONTINUED)

The headlights of a car drive INTO FRAME, illuminating JACK.
He turns to see:

>   LEATHER (O.S.)
>   What's going on ...?

Two white upper class JUVENILE DELINQUENTS — one wearing a
leather jacket, the other a high school windbreaker — get
out of the car. Each is carrying a gallon of gasoline.
LEATHER also carries a bat. JACK is drunk but he is immediately aware of the danger when he spots the gasoline cans.

>   LEATHR
>   I said, what's going on?
>   (walks up to JACK)
>   What are you doing here?

JACK shakes his head and before he knows it, LEATHER shoves
the bat into his gut, sinking JACK to his knees. WINDBREAKER
places the gasoline cans on the bench and begins to unscrew
them.

>   LEATHER
>   (continuing)
>   You shouldn't hang around this
>   neighborhood.

>   JACK
>   (clutching his stomach)
>   I ... I was just leaving.

>   LEATHER
>   People spend a lot of hard earned money
>   for this neighborhood. It's not fair ...
>   looking out their windows to see your
>   ass asleep on the streets ...

>   JACK
>   Yes ... I ... I agree ...

>   LEATHER
>   Good.
>   (to WINDBREAKER)
>   You believe this drunk?

WINDBREAKER shakes his head.

>   LEATHER
>   (continuing)
>   ... Me neither.

>   JACK
>   *No ... No please ...!*

WINDBREAKER hands LEATHER the can. LEATHER raises it above
JACK's head. AS THE GASOLINE SLOWLY LEAKS ONTO A PETRIFIED

(CONTINUED)

JACK, HE SEES A FIGURE MOVING OUT FROM THE DARKNESS.

> FIGURE
> *All hope abandon, ye who enter here!*

Startled, The YOUTHS turn to the shadows.

> LEATHER
> What the — ...

An ARROW with a rubber suction tip comes flying out of the dark and connects with WINDBREAKER's groin.

> WINDBREAKER
>
> AHHH!

A FIGURE stands backlit — mysterious and powerful, noble and fearless. JACK, LEATHER and WINDBREAKER instinctually bond together in the face of this fourth unknown entity.

The FIGURE turns out to be a BUM. Grimy face, tattered layers of clothing beneath a long overcoat, a pork pie hat with a twig sticking out of it like a plume in a helmet of yore. Over his shoulder, a homemade bow and arrow set. Although clearly downtrodden, behind his beaten appearance, there radiates a calm intelligence and strength. There is something distinctly attractive and confident about him. We learn later his name is PARRY; a combination of Don Quixote and Harpo Marx. PARRY stands before them absolutely delighted with himself — hand on hip — beaming with pride.

> PARRY
> Unhand that degenerate — you adolescent
> ass of a one balled donkey!

> LEATHER
> It's just a bum ... You know, there's
> enough in here for the two of you.

> PARRY
> (à la Glinda)
> Ha, ha, ha, ha rubbish ... now begone
> ... before somebody drops a house on
> you! ...

LEATHER walks right up to PARRY.

> LEATHER
> You a fag too?

> PARRY
> *Fag ... a fag you say!? ...*
> *"Curst wolf! Thy fury inward on thyself*
> *Prey and consume thee!"*

> LEATHER
> Fuck you.

(CONTINUED)

PARRY notices a pimple an LEATHER's cheek.

>   PARRY
>   Ooooo ... that looks like it hurts.

HE presses the zit.

>   LEATHER
>   OWWW ... What are you, nuts?!

>   PARRY
>   BINGO! Tell the man what he's won!

WINDBREAKER grabs PARRY, pinning his arms behind him.
WINDBREAKER laughs. PARRY just turns his head and stares
into his eyes, causing WINDBREAKER to feel weird.

>   PARRY
>   I advise you to let us go.

>   LEATHER
>   You advise us!

>   PARRY
>   You're out-numbered, son.

PARRY glances over LEATHER's shoulder. LEATHER turns to see:

A BUM pushing a shopping cart comes out of the darkness. He
is mumbling to himself incoherently. ANOTHER BUM appears
from the dark, unnerving WINDBREAKER. PARRY looks to a THIRD
BUM, stepping out of the dark, menacingly. Taken by
themselves, the BUMS would look harmless and pathetic. But
in the context of their uncharacteristic organization — they
appear frightening.

LEATHER and WINDBREAKER automatically whip out switchblades
and take a "rumble" stance — as if protecting their catch,
JACK. JACK sort of sides with them if for no other reason
than — he's known them longer.

LEATHER tries to remain confident. He laughs.

>   LEATHER
>   Come on! Go for it!
>   What the hell are they gonna do?
>   They can't do nothin'!

>   PARRY
>   *Nothing! They can do nothing! Gentlemen!*

PARRY takes a few steps back and raises his hand.

JACK stands closer to LEATHER and WINDBREAKER, who prepare
themselves for attack.

>   (CONTINUED)

PARRY lowers his hand which acts as a signal for the BUMS.
The BUMS reach into their coats and each pulls out a
FLASHLIGHT, which they shine at each other as THEY sing:

>   THREE BUMS
>   I like New York in June ... How about you?
>   I like a Gershwin tune ... How about you?

JACK, LEATHER and WINDBREAKER are at a loss. The BUMS aren't
getting all the words, but they're definitely in sync.

PARRY lowers his hand proudly. The BUMS keep singing and
turn their flashlights upon JACK, LEATHER and WINDBREAKER —
blinding them to PARRY.

>   WINDBREAKER
>   Shit.

LEATHER brandishes his knife towards the dark spot where he
thinks PARRY stands. But PARRY takes a flying step back. As
he speaks, the BUMS stop singing and *hum* the song.

>   PARRY
>   Son ... There comes a time in every
>   man's life .. and you will learn this,
>   when and if you become men ...

From his hat, PARRY pulls a long tube sock tied at the end
and filled with a softball at the bottom ...

>   PARRY
>   (continuing)
>   ... That there are only three things in
>   this world ya need ...

HE begins to swing the sock over his head — centrifugally
gaining force.

>   PARRY
>   (continuing)
>   ... Respect for all kinds of life, ...
>   the love af another person who you can
>   trust and pork on a regular basis ...
>   and a nice navy blazer ... oh, and one
>   more thing ... always ... keep your eye
>   on the ball!

PARRY releases the "weapon."

The sock flies out of the darkness and, with amazing
accuracy — beans LEATHER on the forehead between his eyes.
HE drops his knife to rub his head. HE sinks out of camera:

>   LEATHER
>   Ow ... ow ... OW!

                                        (CONTINUED)

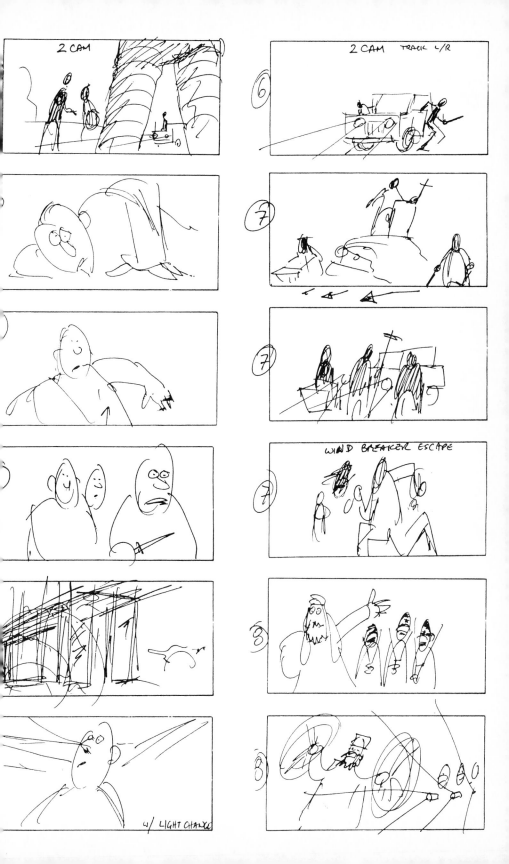

WINDBREAKER grows worried as PARRY reaches into the lining
of his coat, pulls out another "sock weapon" and starts
swinging.

                    PARRY
          Of course, the ability to bean a
          shithead can be a fabulous advantage.

WINDBREAKER runs to the car and drives away. PARRY crosses
to a speechless JACK.

                    PARRY
               (picking up LEATHER's knife)
          Are you all right?

                    LEATHER
               (kneeling, rubbing his head)
          OWW ... MAN ...

                    JACK
               (disoriented)
          Please don't hurt me?

                    PARRY
          "OH beings blind! What ignorance besets
          you!"

PARRY kneels down, pulls out some rope from his coat and
proceeds to tie up LEATHER, who is disoriented and dazed.
PARRY hands JACK LEATHER's knife. Sickened by it, JACK
flings it in the water.

                    LEATHER
          You can't leave me tied up out here
          alone, you fucking faggot!

                    PARRY
               (pulls down LEATHER's pants,
               exposing his butt)
          You won't be alone for long.

PARRY pulls out a triangle and begins ringing it.

                    JACK
          I need a drink.

                    PARRY
          I know a great place.
               (raising his hand HE calls to
               BUM 1)
          ... UH ... WARREN!

                    BUMS (O.C.)
          I like New York in June ... How about — ...

                                        (CONTINUED)

>   PARRY
>   (overlapping)
>   NO ... GUYS ... GUYS ...
>   (to JACK)
>   They're so proud.

CUT TO:

23   **EXT.   A LOT BENEATH THE MANHATTAN BRIDGE — NIGHT**

A violent explosion between the warring factions of BUMS,
who are defending territories and rights ...

CUT TO:

JACK and PARRY sit facing the THREE BUMS from the previous
scene — a BLACK, a MIDDLE-AGED IRISHMAN and an EX-HIPPY —
and the Pinnochio doll. The foursome sit against the giant
base of the bridge discussing the issues of the day as they
pass a bottle. OTHER BUM CLIQUES are scattered throughout
the lot.

>   BLACK
>   ... There ain't no justice in life!
>   There's just satisfaction. And the death
>   penalty's just another violation of my
>   constitutional right to satisfaction,
>   Goddamn it.

>   IRISHMAN
>   (a lit cigarette hangs from his
>   mouth)
>   I hate that.

>   HIPPY
>   So, you mean if somebody like, killed
>   your mother, you wouldn't want him dead?

>   BLACK
>   Sure I would. But I should get to kill
>   him, Goddamn it.

>   IRISHMAN
>   (explaining further)
>   He gets to kill him. That's democracy,
>   see.

A LULL takes over as they all consider this. JACK, sitting
the furthest apart from the group, looks like he's in the
middle of a nightmare.

>   JACK
>   (mumbles to himself)
>   This is it. I'm in hell. Damned to an
>   eternity of idiotic conversation.

(CONTINUED)

> PARRY
> (leans in and smiles)
> Great place, huh?

The IRISHMAN lets out a bloodcurdling scream.

> PARRY
> (responds)
> AAAAHHHH!

JACK jumps. IRISHMAN looks to PARRY and speaks in a calm monotone.

> IRISHMAN
> How are you tonight?

> PARRY
> Fine, John, and you?

> IRISHMAN
> Can't complain.

The IRISHMAN absent-mindedly flicks his cigarette ashes onto JACK's sleeve, which is soaked with gasoline. The SLEEVE IGNITES. JACK panics — waving his arm, trying to get it out. PARRY is both amazed and impressed — seeing it as a sign. The BUMS talk casually as JACK tries to rip off his coat.

> BLACK
> Crazy fuck.

> HIPPY
> (to IRISHMAN)
> So what do you think of the death penalty?

> IRISHMAN
> Death's definitely a penalty. Ain't no fucking gift. Life's too Goddamn short.

With the fire out, JACK tries to leave, saying:

> JACK
> I better be going ...

> IRISHMAN
> (thrusting the bottle at him)
> Have a drink ... don't be shy!

JACK sits quickly.

> PARRY
> I think they like you.

This worries JACK. PARRY retrieves him and brings him back to the group. The IRISHMAN removes the bottle from his

(CONTINUED)

saliva soaked mouth and hands it to JACK, who is disgusted.

> JACK
> Oh no, that's all —

> BLACK
> DRINK! GODDAMN IT!

JACK grabs the bottle and drinks — holding back his nausea.

> PARRY
> Would anyone like a fruit pie?

> THREE BUMS (O.C.)
> No thank you ... too sweet ... too
> fattening ... Goddamn it.

JACK feels sick as the cheap liquor runs through him.
IRISHMAN begins reciting a Chaucer passage in Old English.
The BLACK stares off, half listening. PARRY turns to JACK,
his face beaming, he clasps his hands and says:

> PARRY
> Et in arcadia ego.

> HIPPY
> Man ... why did God invent mediocrity?

This remark acts like a slap in the face to JACK. The others
consider it in silence — not really knowing what it means.
The cheap liquor begins to take its effect and from JACK's
POV, WE FADE OUT OF THE SCENE ON THE NEXT LINES — AS HE
CLOSES HIS EYES AND SLIPS INTO A DRUNKEN SLUMBER.

> HIPPY (O.C.)
> You were phenomonal tonight, Parry!
> (affirmations from the other
> two)
> SUPER-BUM man! Fucking Marvel Comics ...

                                            FADE OUT

FADE-UP ON:

24   INT.   **PARRY'S BASEMENT HIDEAWAY** — MORNING.

JACK is asleep on a mattress beside a boiler spewing steam.
He is slowly awakened by water dripping on his cheek — the
first dull pangs of a mean hangover making itself known. He
opens his eyes, confused — not knowing exactly what
happened.

                                            CUT TO:

THE GIANT FACE OF PARRY lying beside him — like a kid
waiting for his parents to wake up Xmas morning.

                                            (CONTINUED)

                        PARRY
                  (loud and cheery)
            How are you feeling?

Jarred, JACK nods suspiciously. He notices the surroundings.

                        JACK
            Have I died?

                        PARRY
                  (friendly)
            Hahahahaaa ... Nononono ... not yet ...
            hahahaha ...

                        JACK
                  (his head and stomach throbbing)
            If you're going to murder me, that's
            fine ... just don't laugh.

He tries to focus his eyes and looks around the room: there
is an extremely organized "living area" — a makeshift
kitchen with hot plate, a nail in the wall with clothes on
hangers ... there is also a dumpster sitting beneath a
garbage chute — the dumpster has planets and stars painted
on its side.

JACK looks to the far wall and sees a handmade collage
mural: pictures cut out and pasted in a haphazard manner,
all medieval in origin; grassy landscapes with castles,
knight and maidens on horses, crests and symbols of the
Crusades, and various renditions of the Holy Grail. One
maiden stands out from the rest — a frail looking doe-like
creature.

On the adjacent wall, however, there are no pictures. Only
frantic scribblings in red marker. Out of the scribblings we
can see: an evil looking face with a bear amateurishly drawn
... a large red horse drawn as if it hurt to get out of the
image ... the style is violent and erratic.

JACK looks to the other wall and finds PARRY's arsenal —
homemade "weapons" that also look medieval, like lances made
from mop sticks, nets made of knotted rope, slingshots and a
shield made from a garbage can cover with a rose painted on
it. Against each wall are piled what seems to be hundreds of
books. JACK doesn't know what to make of all this. He is
frightened.

                        JACK
            Where am I?

                        PARRY
            My abode ... my domicile ... my neck of
            the woods ... Hungry? Breakfast? A fruit
            pie perhaps?

                                          (CONTINUED)

29

                        JACK
          No ... thanks ... listen —

                        PARRY
          My name is Parry ...

                        JACK
              (realizes he's barefoot)
          Hi ... where are my shoes?

                        PARRY
          They're —
              (suddenly stands)
          — What?

                        JACK
              (jumps)
          Where — ?

                        PARRY
              (to the air)
          What!?

                        JACK
          What?!

                        PARRY
          Sshhhh!

PARRY looks like he's listening to someone. Then he smiles
broadly at JACK, which makes JACK worry even more.

                        PARRY
              (continuing; to the air)
          I knew it! I knew it last night!
              (beat; argues)
          I did too! He's the one!

He kneels beside JACK, which makes JACK lean up against the
boiler.

                        PARRY
              (continuing)
          ... Can you keep a secret?

JACK shakes his head.

                        PARRY
              (continuing)
          Do you know what the Little People just
          told me?

                        JACK
          The Little People?

                        PARRY
          They said you're The One.

                                              (CONTINUED)

>   JACK
>   I'm the one what?

>   PARRY
>   (stands abruptly)
>   *Oh shut up!!!*

He picks up a can of wintergreen air freshener and starts
spraying, with violent strokes, to shut "them" up. JACK gets
more nauseous from the smell. PARRY yells to the air:

>   PARRY
>   (continuing)
>   ... I've got a right to say something. I
>   mean, you're tying my hands here!
>   (to JACK)
>   They say you're not ready to know.

>   JACK
>   I'm not ...
>   (to himself)
>   Now. where are those shoes ...

JACK makes a move to stand when PARRY stops spraying and
yells:

>   PARRY
>   *Hheeyy!!*

JACK sits back down. PARRY whispers to the air:

>   PARRY
>   (continuing)
>   ... You're frightening him!

PARRY kneels before him. JACK presses against the boiler.

>   PARRY
>   (continuing)
>   ... Do you know who I am?

>   JACK
>   Uhh ... I'm drawing a blank.

>   PARRY
>   Take a guess ...
>   (shouts to the air)
>   *Let him guess!! Tch!!*

He goes for the air freshener but JACK's reply stops him.

>   JACK
>   Uh ... gee ... well ... you seem to be
>   some kind of vigilante ...

                                        (CONTINUED)

> PARRY
>
> No, no ... I mean that sort of happens
> along the way, but no ...
> > (proudly)
> I'm on a very special quest.

> JACK
>
> A quest?

> PARRY
>
> But I need help and *they* sent you.

> JACK
> > (clarifying)
> The Little ...

> PARRY
> > (nods)
> They work for Him.

> JACK
>
> Him ...?

> PARRY
> > (leans in to whisper)
> God ... I'm the janitor of God.

JACK's face drops. PARRY gets comfortable and explains casually:

> PARRY
> > (continuing)
> ... *They* came to me about a year ago. I
> was sitting on the john having one of the
> most satisfying bowel movements — you know
> the ones — where you just see God ... and
> I saw them ... just floating around ...
> hundreds of these ... cute little fat
> people ... and they spoke. They said "I"
> was chosen to help get back something very
> important they lost. But my part might be
> very dangerous. I said "Whoah" ... slow
> down ... ya start hearing voices from
> floating little fat people that tell you
> you're on a mission from God and you
> wind up in a mini-series. Then they said
> "Look in *Architecture Today*, Feb '88 ...
> page 33 ..."

PARRY quickley crosses to a pile of magazines, grabs one and dives back to JACK, who keeps scanning for his shoes. PARRY leafs through the magazine and opens to page 33.

> PARRY
> > (continuing)
> And there it was ... plain as day.

(CONTINUED)

He shows JACK a feature about Langdon Carmichael, a Malcolm
Forbes type real estate baron. The five page pictorial
depicts his ten million dollar restoration of an old N.Y.
Armory into a palatial city home. Caption reads: "REAL
ESTATE BILLIONAIRE LANGDON CARMICHAEL'S TOWER OF POWER".

> JACK
> Langdon Carmichael?

Carmichael himself — a dashing bachelor around fifty-five —
is shown standing in his private library beside a glass
commode. PARRY points to inside the commode, where a golden
chalice is displayed.

> PARRY
> It's the Grail ... The Holy Grail.

He indicates the pictures on the collage. JACK's losing it.

> JACK
> The Holy Grail? Some billionaire has the
> Holy Grail sitting in a commode on
> Madison Avenue?

> PARRY
> I know! You can't imagine how surprised
> I was. Who would think you could find
> anything divine on the Upper East Side?

> JACK
> (annoyed now)
> Listen ... I don't mean to be flippant
> or to enrage you or anything but ...
> you're an imbecile. And I'm not The One
> ... I'm not *any* One ...

PARRY tries to speak, but:

> JACK
> (continuing)
> I think you're a very nice ... very nice
> psychotic man. I really appreciate what
> you did for me. It was a brave and noble
> thing ...

> PARRY
> Oh please ... you're embarrassing me.

> JACK
> (rising)
> I wish you all the luck in the world. When
> you get the Grail, I'm sure I'll be seeing
> lots of you on various talk shows ...

> PARRY
> (upset)
> But I can't get it ... He's ...

(CONTINUED)

He runs to the wall with the scribblings in red and
indicates the evil face with the beard. He picks up a red
marker and begins scribbling furiously — adding to the face
and the horse.

                         PARRY
                    (continuing)
          He's out there ... I don't know if ...
          He's always out there, see ... and ...

He drops the marker and smiles to JACK.

                         PARRY
                    (continuing)
          See, you don't know him ... That's why
          you're the one ... You can get it ...

                         JACK
          Listen, forget the shoes. I'll just take
          a cab ... Uh ...

                         PARRY
          Parry.

                         JACK
          Parry ... I'm Jack ...

                         PARRY
          I know ...

PARRY rushes to a corner and gets JACK's shoes and Pinnochio
doll, then rushes to JACK and hands them over.

                         JACK
          Thanks ... You can keep the doll.

                         PARRY
          Thanks a mill —
                  (like a corporate exec)
          And I'll give you a buzz as soon as I
          hear from the people upstairs and we'll
          get this thing off the ground ... Thanks
          for stopping by, Jack. Give my love to
          the wife and kids.

PARRY grabs JACK's hand and shakes it.

                         JACK
          I'm not married.

                         PARRY
          Funny — you look married.

Horrified, JACK makes a hasty exit.

25   INT.   BROWNSTONE HALLWAY — MINUTES LATER

JACK steps out of what appears to be the entrance to the
basement. He walks down the hallway toward the front exit
when suddenly an apartment door swings open. FRANK, a burly
black superintendent with a hearing aid, steps out.

                    FRANK
          Where you comin' from?

                    JACK
          Uh ... basement, I think ...

                    FRANK
               (yells to basement)
          I tell him no visitors!!!

JACK's hangover sets off another explosion.

                    JACK
          Sorry ... I ...

                    WIFE (O.S.)
          Fraaaankkk! Who's at the door?!

JACK glances through the half-opened door and sees the
bottom half of FRANK's wheelchair-bound WIFE: one leg is
normal, the other is a pink prosthetic. Both, however, are
wearing furry mules. JACK's nightmare doesn't seem to end.

                    FRANK
          *I'm talkin' to somebody. Ya gotta yell
          like a banshee?!!*

                    WIFE (O.S.)
          It's just my manner!

                    FRANK
               (hard of hearing)
          What?

                    WIFE (O.S.)
          I said it's just my manner!!!

JACK's head is now nearly split down the middle.

                    FRANK
          You a friend of Parry's?

                    JACK
          No ...
               (trying to clear his vision)
          He is supposed to live there?

                                        (CONTINUED)

>   FRANK
>   Yeah, well ... I let him stay there.
>   What else could I do after such a
>   tragedy?

>   JACK
>   Tragedy?

>   FRANK
>   (dying to tell)
>   He and his wife were at some bar ... and
>   some nut comes in with a shotgun and
>   blew the place apart. She was a beauti-
>   ful girl ... She never knew what hit
>   her.

JACK goes numb. He can't believe his ears. He leans against
the wall for support. CAMERA on JACK as FRANK continues O.S.

>   FRANK (O.S.)
>   (continuing)
>   ... You must have heard about it. That
>   nut who listened to the radio?

LIGHT CHANGE on JACK against the bare wall. (Perhaps even
the scenery is moved behind him) as we fade out FRANK's
voice.

>   FRANK
>   (continuing)
>   Parry's not his real name. His real
>   name's Henry Sa ...

And fade in ANNE's voice.

>   ANNE (V.O.)
>   ... Listen. I understand about open
>   relationships. Please. I was a teenager
>   in the sixties after all ... I
>   understand!

>   CUT TO:

26   INT.   VIDEO SPOT OFFICE — DAY

ANNE sits at her desk, surrounded by her shelves of porno
tapes. JACK sits before her looking like death warmed over.
FRANK's voice reverbs in his head as he half listens to
ANNE.

>   ANNE
>   ... But when you care about somebody ya
>   need more than an open relationship. Ya
>   need a phone call.

Her intercom RINGS. ANNE's tone immediately changes.

>   (CONTINUED)

                              ANNE
                         (continuing)
             WHAT! ...

                         EMPLOYEE (V.O.)

             A guy wants to check out the pornos ...

                              ANNE
             So send him back!
                         (she flicks off the intercom and
                         returns to JACK, softly)
             ... Ya need to pick up the phone and
             tell me that you're not dead ... that
             you haven't been attacked or raped or
             who knows. You disappear last night. I
             don't know what to think. I was up all
             night. Look at you!

A meek, fiftyish BUSINESSMAN has enetered and begins to
browse through the porno videos discreetly.

                              JACK
             I'm sorry.

                              ANNE
             I smell gas ... Do you smell gas ...

She and the BUSINESSMAN exchange glances. JACK is about to
respond when ANNE continues.

                              ANNE
                         (continuing)
             I can't tell you how distraught I was.
             All night long. What the hell happened?

                              JACK
             I was attacked.

                              ANNE
             What!

                              JACK
             Two kids tried to set me on fire.

                              ANNE
             Oh my God ... What did they do! My
             God!!!

She crosses to JACK and hugs him. The BUSINESSMAN turns with
a concerned look, having overheard. JACK indicates to ANNE
that he feels awkward in front of the BUSINESSMAN. ANNE
confronts the BUSINESSMAN with as little tact as possible.

                              ANNE
                         (continuing)
             Are you almost done!?

                                             (CONTINUED)

> BUSINESSMAN
> (flustered)
> Well ...

> ANNE
> Whatta looking for — a story!?
> (makes a selection)
> Here ... "Creamer Versus Creamer" ... It
> won an award.

JACK hides his face so as not to laugh. ANNE ushers the MAN
out.

> ANNE
> (continuing)
> You were attacked. My God. Should I call
> a doctor? Did you call the police ...

> JACK
> No. I'm fine ... really ...

> ANNE
> You're all right ... you sure ...

JACK nods. So, ANNE moves on to more important matters.

> ANNE
> (continuing)
> ... So ... where did you sleep last night?

> JACK
> I ... I stayed at a friend's. Listen, I —

> ANNE
> (puts up her hand)
> Please ... before you go on ... let me
> tawk ... okay ... We've had a wonderful
> time together ... When we first met, you
> said this isn't serious and I shouldn't
> get serious and then you moved in and we
> haven't been serious. And I just wanna
> say that I have no regrets. None. And
> don't wanna have any now so I want ya to
> be up front with me ... I want the
> truth. If you're seein' somebody else,
> let me know ... You don't have to pour
> gasoline on yourself and light a match
> just to break up with me. Just tell me
> the truth.

JACK looks to her — somewhat admiring the bravery and
integrity underneath the peasant stock.

> JACK
> I'm not seeing anyone else. I really was
> attacked.

(CONTINUED)

38

                            ANNE
Okay.
                 (satisfied, she struts to her
                 desk)
... I love you ...

JACK smiles weakly.

                            ANNE
                 (continuing)
... You don't have to say it back ...
although it wouldn't kill you. I'll cook
tonight.

                                      CUT TO:

27   INT.   **ANNE'S APARTMENT ABOVE THE STORE — NIGHT**

ANNE and JACK have just finished eating dinner.

                            JACK
You know what the Holy Grail is?

ANNE takes a long drag on her cigarette then puts it out in
her leftover food. JACK is repelled by the habit.

                            ANNE
The Holy Grail? Yeah ... I know that. It
was like — Jesus' juice glass.

JACK just stares at her.

                            ANNE
                 (continuing)
Oh, I used to be such a Catholic.

                            JACK
You still believe in God?

                            ANNE
Oh sure ... Gotta believe in God.
                 (trying to be intellectual)
But I don't think God made man in his
own image. No. 'Cause most of ... the
bullshit that happens, is because of
men. No, I think man was made out of the
devil's image and women were created out
of God — because women can have babies
which is sorta like creating, and which
also explains why women are attracted to
men, because, let's face it, the devil
is a helluva lot more interesting — I
slept with a few saints and let me tell
you ... Booooorring!!! ...And so the
whole point of life, I think, is for men
                 (MORE)

                                    (CONTINUED)

> ANNE (CONTINUED)
> and women to get married so the devil
> and God can live together and, ya know —
> work it out ...
>> (ANNE moves to him and leans in
>> for a kiss)
> ... Not that we have to get married.

JACK notices a brown spot on her chin and pulls away.

> JACK
> ... You have a little ... uh ...
> something on your face ...

> ANNE
> Oh, I got a pimple ... This stuff is
> supposed to blend with my skin color ...
> Like it really works, ya know ...

JACK moves to the bar to fix a drink. ANNE follows him and
takes the drink out of his hand. JACK knows what this means.

> JACK
> I don't think I'm up to it tonight ...

ANNE massages his shoulders.

> JACK
> I had a very traumatic experience ...
> I ...

ANNE nods, but keeps massaging. As long as he wasn't with a
woman, she doesn't care. Her massaging gets more intense —
moving up his head and contorting his face as he speaks.

> JACK
> (continuing)
> I think I'm getting sick ...
>> (trying to be forceful)
> I ... I slept in a boiler room. Anne ...
> I'm tired ... I'm upset ... I'm ... just
> not in the mood! ... Okay!

ANNE grabs his face with both hands and pulls him into a
kiss. She proceeds to climb onto his body as she utilizes a
skill she picked up in high school make-out parties. She is
a pro. JACK, against all his better judgement and will —
despite the pimple cream — is rendered helpless by this
woman's passion. He returns the embrace and guides her to
the floor.

                                                    CUT TO:

28   INT.   **ANNE'S LIVING ROOM — MIDDLE OF THE NIGHT**

JACK sits in his underwear on the living room floor before

                                              (CONTINUED)

an open closet with a cardboard box between his legs. The
box is filled with tapes of JACK's past radio shows. He
begins to sort through them — reading titles, remembering
moments — then stops when he comes upon newspaper clippings
of the murder at Babbitt's. Edwin Malnick's face stares out
at him from a yellowed front page. The memories sour. He
moves to the bar. ANNE exits the bedroom.

                    ANNE
          Whatsa matter, hon — can't sleep?

She sees the radio tapes.

                    JACK
          I tell you something, Anne. I really
          feel like I'm cursed.

                    ANNE
          Oh stop. Things will change. My Aunt
          Mary always said, there's a remedy for
          everything in this world except death
          and having no class.

                    JACK
          I get the feeling like I'm ... a magnet
          but I attract shit. Out of all the
          people in this city, why did I meet a
          man who's wife I killed?

                    ANNE
          You didn't kill anybody. Stop.

                    JACK
          I wish there was some way I could ...
          just ... pay the fine and go home.

ANNE crosses to JACK and gently touches him. JACK turns and
clutches her to him tightly. Lowering his head to hers, he
cries.

                    ANNE
          I know. I know, honey.

                                        CUT TO:

29   INT.   PARRY'S BASEMENT — THE NEXT DAY

JACK is alone in the basement. He slowly walks around the
room — picking up little items here and there, as if trying
to discover some clue to PARRY. He scans the titles of the
piles of books. All of them have something to do with
medieval history or literature, myths, or the Crusades. He
picks up one of the books and opens it. Page after page has
been ripped out anywhere there might have been a picture or
a diagram. He comes upon a large scroll that he unravels. It
is a map, drawn by PARRY, of Langdon Carmichael's house and

                                        (CONTINUED)

the surrounding blocks. He rolls it up. The Pinnochio doll
sits on a broken chair facing the wall with the nightmarish
scribblings acting like a sentinel.

He crosses to the prominent picture of the maiden with the
long hair. He notices a small stand before the picture, with
a candle. It is like a shrine with offerings: a flower, a
small perfume sampler, a box of Jawbreakers candy and a dime
store romance novel. JACK doesn't understand.

>   FRANK (O.S.)
>   Can I help you?

>   JACK
>   I'm ... just looking for Parry ...

>   FRANK
>   He's not here.

JACK is drawn to the scribblings on the wall and makes out
the faint shape of a man on a horse.

>   JACK
>   What did you say his name used to be?

>   CUT TO:

30   INT.   **FRANK'S APARTMENT — DAY**

CLOSEUP — duffel bag of PARRY's things before JACK.

>   FRANK (O.S.)
>   Hospital said it would be better if we
>   kept certain things away from him.

FRANK speaks O.S. as JACK looks through the items: a
Master's degree in Medieval History, another in Medieval
Literature.

>   FRANK (O.S.)
>   (continuing)
>   ... That's his real name — Henry Sagan.
>   He was a teacher over at Columbia. They
>   kept him in some mental place in Staten
>   Island ... He did not speak for over a
>   year then all of a sudden, he starts
>   talkin' only now he's this Parry guy.

... A torn picture of PARRY in a tux — his wedding ring — a
thesis entitled THE FISHER KING, A MYTHIC JOURNEY FOR MODERN
MAN — FRANK continues:

>   FRANK (O.S.)
>   (continuing)
>   ... He used to live upstairs with his
>   (MORE)

>   (CONTINUED)

>   FRANK (CONTINUED)
>   wife, so when he got released they sent
>   him here. I felt bad. He couldn't work.
>   Nobody wanted him. So I let him stay in
>   the basement. He helps out — I give him
>   a couple of dollars. People throw things
>   away, he gets them.

JACK holds a beautiful photographic portrait of PARRY's
wife.

>   FRANK (O.S.)
>   (continuing)
>   ... She was a beautiful girl. He was
>   crazy about her.

                                                    CUT TO:

31   **EXT.   A LOT BENEATH THE MANHATTAN BRIDGE — DAY**

The BLACK, the IRISHMAN and the HIPPY are in their usual
place. They lean against the wall, observing the afternoon
life that walks by. JACK enters the scene and asks them
where PARRY is. The HIPPY begins to speak and points to his
right. JACK nods in appreciation and hands them a couple of
dollars.

                                                    CUT TO:

32   **EXT.   CORNER OUTSIDE METROPOLOTAN LIFE BUILDING — LATER
      THAT DAY**

JACK approaches PARRY from across the street; he is sitting
on top of a car near a souvlaki vendor and eyeing a clock
tower across the street and to the left of the building. He
studies the time as he recites under his breath (we hear
only excerpts):

>   PARRY
>   "Sovereign princess of this captive
>   heart what dire affliction hast thou
>   made me suffer, thus banished from thy
>   presence with reproach, and fettered by
>   thy rigorous command, not to appear
>   again before thy beautiful face. Deign
>   princess, to remember this thy faithful
>   slave, who now endures such misery for
>   love of thee" ...

>   JACK
>   Parry!

PARRY smiles casually and, without looking at JACK, says:

>   PARRY
>   Hi Jack ...

                                              (CONTINUED)

43

He then returns his gaze to the clock which is approaching
noon. JACK reaches in his pockets and pulls out some money.

>   JACK
>   Hi. Listen ... I thought maybe you could
>   use a —

The CLOCK STRIKES NOON. PARRY grabs JACK.

>   PARRY
>   COME ON!

He pulls JACK into the building.

33   INT.   MET LIFE BUILDING — NOON

Several business men and women make their way out of the
elevators for lunch. PARRY and JACK position themselves with
a clear view of the center elevator. The doors open and
after several more aggressive co-workers exit, PARRY's
DAMSEL in distress appears out of a revolving door, but
quickly gets "revolved" back into the building.

>   PARRY
>   She'll be back ...

Finally, LYDIA makes an exit.

>   PARRY
>   Isn't she a vision?

Reaction shot of a bewildered JACK as he looks at LYDIA — a
dowdy, waif-like sparrow of a thing — makes her way through
the lobby. She is torturously self-conscious, clumsy, form-
less and plain. She wears loose frocks that give her no
shape and make her appear to be swimming in material. She
wears no makeup; her unstyled hair is kept off her face by a
beret that keeps sliding down her head, and her contact
lenses are always dry, causing her to blink and use drops.

>   JACK
>   Yeah, gorgeous ... Look I'm going. I
>   just wanted to give you ...

Stars to dig in his pocket, but PARRY is already off.

>   PARRY
>   Let's go.

JACK follows.

                                              CUT TO:

44

34   EXT.   CHINESE RESTAURANT — DAY

Behind the glass in interior, we can see LYDIA sitting by
herself eating lunch. CAMERA pans out to the street where
PARRY and JACK are sittting on the hood of a car, watching.

                    PARRY
          She loves dumplings. It's her Wednesday
          ritual.

LYDIA raises a dumpling to her lips with a pair of
chopsticks. She then accidentally drops it into a dish of
soy sauce and splatters her dress. Unnerved, she hastily
wipes herself down, knocking over a glass of water when she
removes the napkin.

                    PARRY
               (continuing)
          Isn't she sweet. She does that every
          time ...

JACK squints at LYDIA as if trying to see what PARRY sees.

                                        CUT TO:

35   EXT.   BOOKSTAND NEAR GRAND CENTRAL STATION — DAY

JACK and PARRY have followed LYDIA into a bookstore. She
stands browsing through a revolving bookstand. They watch
from a distance.

                    PARRY
          She buys a new book every two days.

LYDIA spins too hard, sending books flying off. She replaces
the books, but keeps one called Loves Lusty Longings ...

                    PARRY
               (continuing; smiles with great
               affection)
          She's into trash. Whadda you gonna do?

                                        CUT TO:

36   EXT.   MET LIFE BUILDING — DAY

PARRY and JACK are following LYDIA, when she stops at a
newsstand.

                    PARRY
          She's got a real sweet tooth. If anybody
          ever told me I'd be in love with a woman
          who eats jawbreakers, I'd say they were
          nuts.
               (reverentially)
               (MORE)

                                        (CONTINUED)

45

> PARRY (CONTINUED)
> But look at that jaw!

JACK doesn't want to look. If the Little People made PARRY
seem crazy, this infatuation confirms him as beyond hope.

CUT TO:

37   EXT.   MET LIFE BUILDING — DAY

LYDIA buys some candy then turns and walks back toward her
office building, once again waiting her turn to dive into
the revolving doors. She disappears into the building.

> JACK
> Do you follow her every day?

> PARRY
> Uh-huh. I'm deeply smitten.

> JACK
> Who is she? What's her name?

> PARRY
> I don't know.

A BUSINESSMAN, walking in the opposite direction, throws a
candy wrapper on the street as he passes JACK and PARRY.
PARRY suddenly stops, outraged, pulls out a slingshot and
fires a stone at the MAN's head. The BUSINESSMAN is hit but
doesn't know how, since PARRY grabs JACK's arm and resumes
walking casually in the opposite direction.

> JACK
> Why did you do that?

> PARRY
> Well, if every time somebody did
> something offensive they got hit in the
> head with a pebble, I think they might
> alter their behavior. What do you think,
> Jack ...

Before JACK can respond, PARRY spots a rummage find:

> PARRY
> Oh look! A cooler!

PARRY spots an abandoned cooler filled with junk and starts
going through it. Things are getting weird again, so JACK
seizes the moment to accomplish his initial task — he pulls
out a fifty dollar bill and hands it to PARRY.

> JACK
> Here ... I just would like to help you.
> I thought ... maybe ... you could use
> some money.

(CONTINUED)

>   PARRY
>   Fifty dollars?

JACK digs deeper and hands him a twenty. PARRY is
dumbfounded.

>   JACK
>   Here's another twenty. Will that do?
>   (sorting through his change)
>   I mean, what's it going to take! ...

>   PARRY
>   No ... no, it's ... I don't know what to
>   say. This is so nice of you ... Jack ...

He hugs him on the street which embarrasses JACK to no end.

>   JACK
>   (pulling away)
>   That's O.K.

>   PARRY
>   Can I take you to lunch?

>   JACK
>   No ... I have to get back to work. Take
>   care of yourself.

JACK walks away. CAMERA stays on JACK for a few yards until
he turns around and sees PARRY handing the money to a BUM in
a doorway, yelling into an imaginary phone.

>   BUM
>   SELL! ... SELL! ... SELL! ...
>   (he takes the money from PARRY)
>   BUY! ... BUY! ... BUY! ...

>   JACK
>   HEY!! ... HEY!

JACK walks back to PARRY, who is explaining to the BUM, who
is now talking gibberish.

>   PARRY
>   (as if he understands)
>   Well, I think you should be realistic.
>   Ya can't start an ad agency on fifty
>   dollars!

>   JACK
>   What are you doing?
>   (to BUM)
>   Give that back!

The BUM screams in defiance. PARRY pulls JACK away.

>   (CONTINUED)

                              JACK
          But I gave it to you!

                             PARRY
          Well what am I going to do with it?

                              JACK
          I don't know. But I gave it to you ...
          to help YOU ... not him.

                             PARRY
                    (beat, then smiles
                    mischieviously)
          You really want to help me?

     A wary JACK, who's afraid to reply.

                                                    CUT TO:

38   EXT: **LANGDON CARMICHAEL'S TOWNHOUSE — DAY**

     On the Upper East Side, PARRY and JACK stand across the
     tree-lined street from the ten million dollar armory/house.

                             PARRY
          Pretty impressive, huh? ... Don't let it
          scare you. I'll admit it's formidable
          but everything has its weakness.

                              JACK
          You can't just break into Langdon
          Carmichael's house. This man has done
          nothing.

                             PARRY
          O.K. ... let me explain this one more
          time ... The Holy Grail is in —

                              JACK
          All right! Listen — please ... don't
          start drooling or ... rolling your eyes
          when I tell you this but — You shouldn't
          be doing this. There is no Holy Grail.

                             PARRY
          Of course there is, Jack. What do you
          think the Crusades were — a frat
          initiation? I don't think so ... There
          has to be a Grail.

                              JACK
          Look, you're only sort of insane,
          really. People like you can lead semi-
          normal lives. You could get a job ...

                             PARRY
          I don't need a job. I have a quest

                                              (CONTINUED)

                         JACK
          I take it back — you're fucking deranged
          ... And you're going to get yourself
          killed trying to get in there!

                         PARRY
          Tch. You are so sweet ... Now I know why
          you're saying this ... You're afraid
          there's danger and you're trying to
          protect me.

                         JACK
          No. I think you're a moron and I don't
          want to get into trouble.

Ignoring this, PARRY gets filled with emotion and hugs JACK.

                         PARRY
          ... You are such a great guy. First the
          money, now this.
                    (to the LITTLE PEOPLE)
          Isn't he fabulous!?

                         JACK
                    (pulling away)
          Please don't hug me in public again, O.K.?

                         PARRY
                    (shouts)
          I LOVE THIS MAN ... YA HEAR ME JADED
          CITY ...
                    (JACK is mortified)
          ... I'M DAFFY ABOUT THIS GUY AND I DON'T
          CARE WHO KNOWS IT!!!

A COUPLE passes by, obviously not wanting to know it.

                         JACK
          Will you shut up!!!

                         PARRY
          You're a true *friend*.

                         JACK
          I'm not. Believe me. *I'm* scum.

                         PARRY
          You're a real honest to goodness *good*
          guy.

                         JACK
          I'm self-centered, I'm weak — I don't
          have the will power of a fly on shit ...

                         PARRY
          That's why the Little People sent you.
          Just *like* magic.

                                        (CONTINUED)

                         49

                              JACK
              I don't believe in little floating
              people! THERE IS NO MAGIC!

                              PARRY
              So what? You going to help me?

                      JACK
         WILL YOU PLEASE ... please
         listen to me ...
              (he grabs PARRY
              by the shoulders)
         You know none of this is true —   PARRY
         the Grail, the voices ...   Jack ...
         There's a part of you that   Come on ... what are
         knows this isn't true.   you saying ...
              I know who you are ...   I know who you are ...
                   or who you were.   You're acting really —
                   You don't belong on the No, no, no, no ...
         streets. You're intelligent   Jack ...
         man. ... You're a teacher ...   Jacck! ...
         You were a teach at Hunter College.
         Con't you remember?   (SCREAMS)

PARRY breaks away from him. He falls back onto the ground.
THE SCREAM STOPS and is replaced by an eerie SILENCE, as if
sound were ripped out of space. JACK speaks but no sound
comes out. We are in PARRY's world for this brief moment.
JACK leans over to help PARRY, but the latter inches away,
fearful of the vision he sees: something out of sight,
looming over JACK, breathing FIERY SMOKE. JACK tries to
raise PARRY off the ground and, in doing so, the vision for
PARRY comes into full view.

                                                      CUT TO:

38A   A MAGNIFICENT BURNISHED RED STEED

Stares down at PARRY. On top of him sits the RED KNIGHT — a
helmeted figure with a beard in a flowing red cap, holding a
lance. He stares at PARRY. Closing his eyes, PARRY raises
his hands to protect himself.

JACK looks around and sees nothing. He acts with great
concern.

                          JACK
                   (mouthing in silence)
              Parry ... you all right?

He embraces PARRY by the shoulders. PARRY turns to him
opening his eyes, then turns back to the KNIGHT to discover
that the HORSE and the KNIGHT have moved several feet away,

                                                  (CONTINUED)

and are continuing to back up ... as if in retreat.

JACK speaks as the sound is returned.

>   JACK
>   Parry answer me ... are you all right?

PARRY smiles in amazement.

>   PARRY
>   He knows who you are!
>   (amazed)
>   He's afraid! I can tell!

>   JACK (O.S.)
>   You're totally gone, aren't you?

                                        CUT TO:

THE RED KNIGHT. He pulls the reins back, forcing the horse
up onto its hind legs. Then, he gallops off.

                                        CUT TO:

PARRY AND JACK

>   PARRY
>   *We've got 'em ... come on!!!*

PARRY runs O.S. in the direction of the KNIGHT. JACK is not
about to follow, until he sees PARRY running into the
intersection of 74th and Fifth, almost getting hit by a cab.

>   JACK
>   Jesus.

JACK runs after him.

                                        CUT TO:

39   EXT.   FIFTH AVE. AND 74TH — DAY

PARRY reaches where the RED KNIGHT stood and looks.

                                        CUT TO:

THE RED KNIGHT riding onto the sidewalk and into Central
Park.

                                        CUT TO:

PARRY as JACK reaches him.

>   JACK
>   What is going o —

Before he can finish, PARRY is off again. JACK races after
him.

40   EXT.   CENTRAL PARK — DAY

They climb the wall and run into the park. They dodge past
women with strollers, runners, bikers, sun worshippers, etc.
They run deep through an extremely woody section of Central
Park. The RED KNIGHT appears first to the left, then
re-appears to the right. PARRY darts about like a madman.

40A   EXT.   ROCK — CENTRAL PARK — DAY

The RED KNIGHT is perched atop a rock. He and PARRY exchange
looks. The KNIGHT and his HORSE rear up, two towering figures
against the Central Park South skyline.

40B   EXT.   CENTRAL PARK — DAY

PARRY, uttering a war cry, rushes off again.

40C   EXT.   ROCK — CENTRAL PARK — DAY

JACK, exhausted and bedraggled, climbs the rock to follow.
He reaches the top, panting.

                    JACK
          Oh ... oh ... oh God ... I'm dying. I
          can't breathe and I'm dying.

He finds PARRY sitting Buddha-like, on the top of the rock,
calmly gazing out at the beautiful scenery before him.

                    PARRY
          Isn't it great up here ... He's gone
          now, but we had him on the run! We
          would've had his ass if we had horses!
          He's running scared!

                    JACK
          WHO! WHO'S RUNNING!! WHO HAVE WE BEEN
          CHASING!?? CAN I ASK THIS QUESTION
          NOW!!!

CAMERA PANS BACK SLOWLY from behind JACK and PARRY.

                    PARRY
          I'm sorry, Jack. I thought you saw him.

CAMERA reveals the head of HORSE.

                    JACK
          SAW WHO!!?

                                        (CONTINUED)

                                    PARRY
                        The Red Knight!

                                    JACK
                        The Red ...?
                                (stares at him in wonder)
                        You're totally gone, aren't you?

Frustrated, JACK turns to leave but this time there is a
sound — someone is crying O.S.

                                    PARRY
                        ... Do you hear that!? Oh "Heaven be
                        praised, in giving me an opportunity, so
                        soon of fulfilling the duties of my
                        profession ... These cries doubtless
                        proceed from some miserable male or
                        female, who stands in need of my
                        immediate aid and protection!"

And he's off. A reluctant JACK pauses before following.

                                    JACK
                        This is too hard.

                                                            CUT TO:

42   EXT.   CENTRAL PARK — BRIDLE PATH — DAY

A BEATEN MAN cries as he sits in the middle of the dirt
bridle path — mumbling to himself, trying to bury himself in
dirt. He hears the TWO MEN coming.

                                    GAY BUM
                        GET AWAY! GET AWAY!! ...

PARRY kneels down to him. JACK keeps a safe distance away.

                                    PARRY
                        It's O.K. ... It's O.K. ... Let me help
                        you up.

                                    GAY BUM
                        NO ... I WANNA GO! I WANNA GO NOW!

                                    PARRY
                        Come on now ... you can't sit here.

                                    GAY BUM
                        NO! I want a debutante on a horse to
                        step on me. Leave me alone!!

                                    JACK
                                (wanting to leave)
                        Parry ...

                                                        (CONTINUED)

                         PARRY
          Buddy, the days of the debutantes are
          ... not what they used to be.

                         GAY BUM
                    (starts to cry)
          Isn't that awful? Poor Brenda Frazier.
          Poor little Gloria. They ruined them!
          THEY ATE THEM ALIVE!

                         PARRY
                    (helping him up)
          It was a crime.

                         GAY BUM
          Leave me alone ... I wanna go ...

PARRY lifts him up — he looks to JACK for help.

                         PARRY
          Will you get the other side?
                    (JACK hesitates)
          Jack?

The MAN's cuts and suicidal demeanor turn JACK off.

                         JACK
          Listen, he just needs to sleep it off.
          Someone will take care of him.

                         PARRY
          Who?

                         JACK
          Well, maybe he wants to stay here.
                    (to BUM)
          Do ... do you want to stay here?

                         GAY BUM
                    (suddenly lucid and pissy)
          Oh yes, thank you — I really love
          bleeding in horseshit. How very
          Gandhiesque of you.

PARRY looks to JACK, who then begrudgingly helps the BUM up.

                                        CUT TO:

43   INT.   EMERGENCY ROOM — LATER

In a room at the end of the line of chairs, PARRY stands
holding the GAY BUM. JACK stands a safe distance away,
unable to take his eyes off the scene before him: seated
against the wall are an assortment of derelicts, drunks,
screaming withdrawal victims and jacketed schizophrenics.
JACK has a hard time moving.

                                        (CONTINUED)

>   PARRY
>   (to JACK, referring to the GAY
>   BUM)
>   Will you watch him for a minute?

Before JACK can respond, PARRY shifts the GAY BUM's body
into JACK's arms, then moves about the room, introducing
himself to the various patients as JACK watches. He moves
down the line, saying hello, wiping people's brows, holding
the hands of an angry BAG LADY mumbling incoherently.
Smiling and saying hello to each one, no matter how
frightening they seem. He appears to have a soothing effect.

>   GAY BUM
>   I wanna go ... Just let me go ...

JACK leads the GAY BUM to two vacant seats. Inspired by
PARRY, JACK tries to be nice to the GAY BUM.

>   JACK
>   Uh ... where ... where do you want to
>   go?

>   GAY BUM
>   A real nice place I know ... Ah ...
>   can't get there! Not tonight.

>   JACK
>   Where? Maybe we can.

>   GAY BUM
>   (overlapping, crying)
>   No ... no ... we can't ... we can't ...

>   JACK
>   (with more feeling)
>   Come on ... maybe we can ... where do
>   you want to go?

>   GAY BUM
>   Venice ... like Katharine Hepburn in
>   *Summertime.*
>   (the GAY BUM cries in
>   frustration)
>   ... Why can't I be Katharine Hepburn ...

JACK stares at him, at a complete loss for a response.

>   GAY BUM
>   I wanna die ... I just wanna die ...

JACK, against all better judgement, pats the BUM's hand in
comfort. Unexpectedly, the GAY BUM leans his head on JACK's
shoulder and cries. JACK, wide-eyed with embarrassment,
looks over to PARRY.

44   INT.   **EMERGENCY ROOM — DAY**

PARRY is teaching a song to a SCHIZO, a YUPPIE IN A STRAIGHT
JACKET and a paranoid BAG LADY.

>   PARRY
>   O.K. ... everyone know their parts ...
>   Here we go ...
>   (sings)
>   "I like New York in June ..."

He points to the YUPPIE who replies:

>   YUPPIE
>   "How about you ..."

>   PARRY
>   "I like a Gershwin tune ..."

PARRY points to the SCHIZO, who stares at him blankly,
drooling.

>   PARRY
>   ... Good! ... "I like to read good
>   books ..."

He points to the BAG LADY, who is talking to herself:

>   BAG LADY
>   Where the hell am I gonna put the
>   children? Goddamn daughter-in-law! Comes
>   into my house looking for dustballs! GET
>   THE FUCK OUTTA MY DINING ROOM ... you
>   ingrate!

>   PARRY
>   Tempo, people ... tempo ...

45   INT.   **EMERGENCY ROOM — DAY**

JACK, his arms around the despairing GAY MAN, is sharing his
problems.

>   JACK
>   Can you tell me something? Did you lose
>   your mind all of a sudden or was it a
>   slow, gradual process?

>   GAY BUM
>   (suddenly coherent)
>   Well, ... I'm a singer by trade ...
>   (MORE)

(CONTINUED)

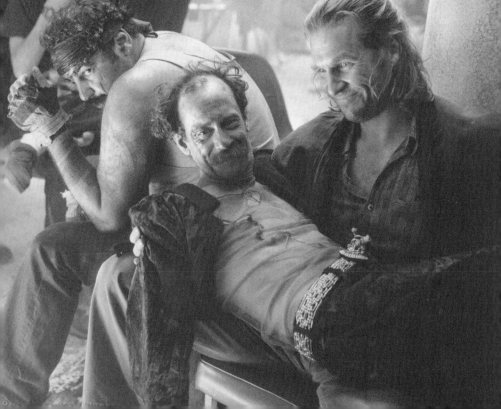

> GAY BUM (CONTINUED)
> Summer stock ... nightclub revues ...
> that kind of thing ... It used to be
> what I absolutely lived for ... God ...
> I can do *Gypsy* backwards — every part —
> but, one night ... in the middle of
> singing "Funny" ... — it suddenly hit me
> ... what does all of this really mean?
> (JACK nods in a knowing
> metaphysical agreement)
> That, and the fact that all my friends
> are dead ... God, I sound like a
> veteran. Dad would be so proud.

At that moment a PIZZA BOY enters, making a delivery.

> PIZZA BOY

Pizza!

Suddenly, DOCTORS and NURSES appear out of the woodwork and
swarm all around the DELIVERY BOY.

CUT TO:

45A   INT.   EMERGENCY ROOM — DAY

PARRY notices the time, passing by the DOCTORS and pizza.

> PARRY
> Jack, it's almost five. We're going to
> be late. We're going to miss her!

PARRY exits. JACK turns to the GAY BUM, exhaustedly.

> JACK
> Uh ... I've got to run. I've been doing
> this all day. Are you going to be all
> right?

> GAY BUM
> Oh please! I was born a Catholic in
> Brooklyn ... I've been to hell and back
> ... I'll be fine ...
> (adds quite sincerely)
> ... Thanks ... You're a gem.

JACK nods, a little self-consciously, and exits.

CUT TO:

46   INT.   GRAND CENTRAL STATION — A BANK — RUSH HOUR

PARRY and JACK sit on the floor enjoying a cup of coffee. A
legless VIETNAM VET in a wheelchair sits near the opposite
wall along with at least fifteen other homeless BEGGARS.

(CONTINUED)

Another MAN sits against a cash machine, crying. A WOMAN passes by and drops some change in the VET's cup without saying a word. The VET, SID, smiles broadly.

> SID
> *God bless you ... Have a nice day.*
> (to JACK and PARRY)
> Ya hear Jimmy Nickels got picked up
> yesterday ...

PARRY is too busy scanning the Grand Central main floor to answer. Realizing PARRY isn't answering, JACK feels obliged to pick up the conversation.

> JACK
> Oh yeah?

> SID
> He got caught —
> (passer-by drops coins in cup)
> God bless ... Have a safe trip home ...
> (to JACK)
> — Got caught pissin' on the bookstore.
> Man's a pig. No excuse for that. We're
> heading for social anarchy when people
> start pissing on bookstores!

JACK smiles at this observation. He then tries to get PARRY's attention.

> JACK
> You'll never see her in this crowd.

PARRY doesn't answer. He looks like a dog waiting for its master. People walk by JACK at a frantic pace. He sits uncomfortably against a wall. A MAN almost steps on him as he walks by and tosses a coin at SID, missing the cup and forcing SID to bend over ... JACK picks the coin up for him.

> SID
> Bless you ...

> JACK
> Asshole! Guy didn't even look at you.

> SID
> (takes coin)
> He's paying so he don't have to look.
> What he doesn't know is, he's paying for
> a service. Guy goes to work every day
> and for eight hours, seven days a week,
> he bends over a gets it right up the ass
> till he can't stand ...

PARRY stands up and begins pacing before the main floor.

(CONTINUED)

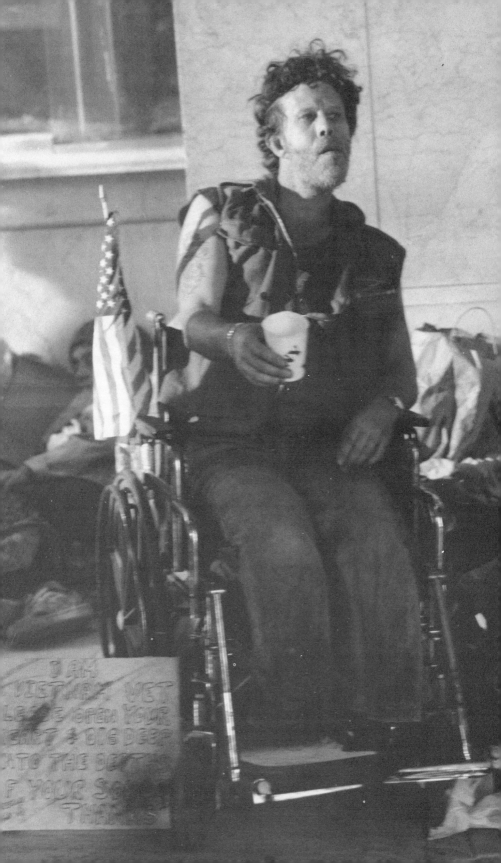

>   SID
>   (continuing)
>   ... But one day, right before quitting
>   time on Friday, his boss is going to say
>   something like "Say Bob — come into my
>   office and kiss my ass" ... and Bob is
>   going to think — "The hell with it! I
>   don't care what happens. All I want
>   right now is to see the expression on
>   his face when I stab him with this pair
>   of scissors" ...

PARRY looks at the clock above the information booth — 5:00.

>   SID
>   (continuing)
>   ... But then he thinks of me — "Wait a
>   minute!" he says, "It's not so bad. At
>   least I got two arms and two legs and I
>   ain't beggin' for money." He puts down
>   the scissors and puckers up ...

JACK is impressed with this man.

>   SID
>   (continuing)
>   ... I'm what you call a moral traffic
>   light. It's like I'm saying "*Red* — go no
>   further."

O.S. a BLACK WOMAN begins to sing. JACK and SID look.

>   SID
>   (continuing; smiles with
>   respect)
>   Ah, Margaret.

>   CUT TO:

47   INT.   GRAND CENTRAL STATION — PHOTO LAB — RUSH HOUR

MARGARET, a black woman in a paisley kaftan, stands near a
photo lab across from JACK and SID. With a box in front of
her for donations, she starts singing (SONG to be chosen).
Some rush hour COMMUTERS stop to listen. Her VOICE is strong
and soulful, and she performs uninhibitedly.

>   SID
>   You have to admit though ... Life at
>   5:00 in Grand Central ... Pretty
>   breathtaking, don't cha think?

JACK looks around this mad rush hour scene, taking it in
through SID's eyes. PARRY, however, keeps his gaze on the
main floor. Suddenly, he spots her.

48   **INT.   GRAND CENTRAL STATION — MAIN FLOOR**

Hordes of people are moving in every which way, zigzagging across the floor. LYDIA moves through the crowd, avoiding touching anyone.

48A   **PARRY**

CAMERA pans in SLOWLY as we hear MARGARET's song O.S. The closer the CAMERA gets to PARRY the more her song changes. At first a blend of two melodies that sound disruptive, cacophonous. But as PARRY smiles with joy, his song overtakes MARGARET's. It is a waltz.

CUT TO:

48B   **MAIN FLOOR —PARRY'S POV**

The hordes of people continue their zigzagging for a beat then:

Suddenly, they pair up and waltz around the main floor, circling around the center information booth.

Only LYDIA remains walking — gliding through the dancers with grace and ease.

PARRY watches in a state of rapture — moving as she moves to keep her in eye view as long as possible.

CUT TO:

48C   **JACK**

listening to MARGARET's SONG, taking in the scene around him, watching people listen to her song, while others walk by as if they were deaf and blind.

Feeling strangely at ease, strangely a part of everyone around him — a group of lost souls listening to a woman bare her soul in song. He looks to PARRY, rises as crosses to him.

CUT TO:

48D   **MAIN FLOOR**

PARRY watches as LYDIA exits the main floor (the waltz has ended) just as JACK speaks his line:

                JACK
   It's such a great song.

                PARRY
         (referring to his own song)
   It's a classic.

(CONTINUED)

JACK looks in the direction of PARRY's stare and sees LYDIA exit.

> PARRY
> (continuing)
> God. Just one night with her. I'd die happy.

JACK hears this as if a light bulb went off above his head.

CUT TO:

49   INT.   LYDIA'S APARTMENT — DUSK

A door opens. LYDIA enters with a bag of groceries she picked up on the way home. She turns on the light to reveal an extremely neat, albeit modest, one bedroom apartment. She carries the grocery bag into the kitchen.

Out of the bag, she removes a Lean Cuisine, a giant bottle of cream soda and four giant bars of chunky chocolate. She pops the Lean Cuisine into the oven and walks back into the living room to an old stereo. She turns the TURNTABLE on — a record already set upon it. She stands by her coffee table, as if taking position.

Suddenly, we hear ETHEL MERMAN — as LYDIA lip-syncs every word with complete commitment — giving a full out performance.

> ETHEL/LYDIA
> Got no sunshine, got no rain
> Still I think I'm a lucky dame
> I got the sun in the morning
> And the moon at night ...

Her attempts at hand gestures and choreography are awkward — bumping into the coffee table, banging her head against a lamp — but, we see a part of LYDIA that few (actually no one) sees. Her abandon, her joy, her smile. From upstairs, neighbors bang for her to keep the music down. LYDIA casually crosses to the stereo, turns off the turntable and heads back to the kitchen — as if the neighbor's interference was all a part of her nightly ritual.

CUT TO:

50   INT.   ANNE'S APARTMENT — NIGHT

ANNE sits alone at her formica table, smoking a cigarette. Two plates are set. She waits for JACK. She is hurt and pissed off. TONY ORLANDO AND DAWN play on her stereo.

> TONY ET AL
> Knock three times ... on the ceiling if
> you want me ... Twice on the pipes ...

(CONTINUED)

61

The SONG continues as the CAMERA SLOWLY PANS up to closeup of ANNE, who is fighting with an imaginary JACK.

> ANNE
> Ya fuckin' bastard. I don't need
> this ...
> > (emphasizing)
> ... I Do Not Need This! A woman my age
> ... I am a person. This is kid stuff.
> You come! You go! And all I do is cook
> like a jerk! You're a waste of good
> cutlets ... I don't need this ... Find
> yourself another dope ... ya fuckin'
> bastard ...

She puffs on her cigarette.

                                        CUT TO:

51   EXT.   **CENTRAL PARK — SHEEPS MEADOW — NIGHT**

> PARRY
> What a beautiful night.

He walks deeper into the field. This makes JACK nervous.

> JACK
> Don't you think it's time to go now?
> Running around here during the day is
> one thing, but at night we could be
> killed by a wide variety of people.

> PARRY
> Well that's stupid. This is my park just
> as much as it is theirs. You think it's
> fair they keep us out just because they
> make us think we'll get killed or
> something?

> JACK
> Yes. I think that's very fair.

PARRY takes off his pants and stands there naked.

> JACK
> > (continuing)
> ... What are you doing?

> PARRY
> Have you ever done any cloudbusting? You
> lie on your back and you concentrate on
> the clouds ... and you try to break them
> apart with your mind. It's wild.

PARRY lies down.

                                        (CONTINUED)

                        JACK
          You can't do this! This is New York!
          Nobody lies naked in a field in New
          York. It's ... it's too Midwestern.

                        PARRY
          Come on, try it. Ya feel the air on your
          body — ya little fella's flappin' in the
          breeze ... everybody in the city is busy
          with their business and no one knows
          we're bare assed in the middle of it.
          Come on!

                        JACK
          NO! I will not! This is nuts! I'm
          leaving! I mean it ... this is nuts.
                    (freaked, walking O.C.)
          This is too nuts ... I'm leaving! I mean
          it!

JACK starts walking away from PARRY, talking to himself.

                        JACK
          ... Ha ... little fella? I mean the man
          talks to invisible people — he sees
          invisible horses — and he's naked in the
          middle of Central Park. I should be
          surprised? I'm not surprised. I'm
          fucking outta my mind to even be here!

                        PARRY (O.S.)
          Who are you talking to, Jack?

                        JACK
                    (turns back and yells)
          YOU'RE OUT OF YOUR FUCKING MIND!!

                        PARRY (O.S.)
          Bingo!

JACK walks O.S.

                                           CUT TO:

52   **EXT.   CENTRAL PARK — SHEEPS MEADOW — TEN MINUTES LATER —
      NIGHT**

JACK, fully clothed, lies next to PARRY looking up at the
clouds.

                        JACK
          They're not moving.

They stare up. JACK raises his head. He unbuttons his shirt
— maybe that will help.

                                           (CONTINUED)

> JACK
> What if some homophobic jogger runs by
> and kills us to get back at his
> overbearing father?

PARRY remains focused on the sky — in his own world.
Something about cloudbusting makes PARRY behave in a way we
haven't seen before. He is uncharacteristically quiet.

> JACK
> "JACK LUCAS FOUND DEAD — BESIDE A DEAD
> NAKED MAN ... THE TWO WERE DEAD ... HIS
> COMPANION WAS NAKED" ... I hate when
> they use the word companion ... It's so
> insinuating ... Although, it'll probably
> boost my biography sales. The public
> loves stories about successful people
> falling into degenerate behavior. Makes
> them feel lucky to be boring and
> ordinary ... People stink.

PARRY speaks suddenly, as if talking to a lecture hall.

> PARRY
> Are there any questions?

> JACK
> What?

> PARRY
> (continuing)
> Then let's begin with the story itself.
> It's a story of the Grail myth ... and
> although there are several variations,
> my favorite begins with the Fisher King
> as a young boy ... who had to spend a
> night alone in the forest to prove his
> courage ... and during that night, he is
> visited by a sacred vision. Out of the
> fire appears the Holy Grail — God's
> highest symbol of divine grace. And a
> voice says to the boy, "You shall be the
> guardian of the Grail, that it may heal
> the hearts of men" ... But the boy was
> overcome ... Innocent and foolish, he
> was blinded by greater visions — a life
> ahead filled with beauty and glory, hope
> and power ... Tears filled his eyes as
> he sensed his own ... invincibility. A
> boy's tears of naïve wonder and
> inspiration. And in this state of ...
> radical amazement ... he felt for a
> brief moment, not like a boy, but like
> God ...
> (MORE)

(CONTINUED)

                    PARRY (CONTINUED)
                  (JACK listens intently)
... And so he reached into the fire to
take the Grail. And the Grail vanished.
And the boy's hands were left caught in
the flames ... leaving him wounded and
ashamed at what his recklessness had
lost him. When he became King, he was
determined to reclaim his destiny and
find the Grail ... But with each year
that passed, with each campaign he
fought, the Grail remained lost, and
this wound he suffered in the fire grew
worse ... He became a bitter man. Life
for him lost its reason. With each
disappointment, with each betrayal ...
with each loss ... this wound would grow
... Soon the land began to spoil from
neglect and his people starved ... Until
finally, the King lost all faith in
God's existence and in man's value ...
He lost his ability to love or be loved
and he was so sick with experience ...
that he started to die. As the years
went on, his bravest knights would
search for the Grail that would heal
their King and make them the most
respected and valued men in the land,
but to no avail. Pretty soon, finding
the Grail became a ruthless struggle
between ambitious men vying for the
King's power, which only confirmed the
King's worst suspicions of man, causing
his wound to grow. His only hope, he
thought, was death. Then one day, a fool
was brought in to the King to cheer him.
He was a simple-minded man ... not
particularly skilled ... or admired ...
He tells the King some jokes ... sings
him some songs, but the King feels even
worse ... Finally, the fool says, "What
is it that hurts you so much? How can I
help?" ... And the King says, "I need a
sip of water to cool my throat." ... So,
the fool takes a cup from the bedstand,
fills it with water and hands it to the
King ... Suddenly, the King feels a lot
better. And when he looks to his hands,
he sees that it was the Holy Grail the
fool handed him ... an ordinary cup that
had been beside his bed all along ...
And the King asks, "How can this be? ...
How could you find what all my knights
                    (MORE)

                                    (CONTINUED)

> PARRY (CONTINUED)
> and wisest men could not find?" And the
> fool answers, "I don't know. I only knew
> you were thirsty." ... And for the first
> time since he was a boy, The King felt
> more than a man — not because he was
> touched by God's glory ... but rather,
> by the compassion of a fool.

JACK doesn't know how to respond. He's never known PARRY to
be so eloquent. He gets a glimpse of PARRY as he once was
and the words come out of his mouth before he knows it:

> JACK
> I'm so sorry.

But PARRY seems far away. He speaks like a professor:

> PARRY
> The Fisher King myth has a lot of
> derivations ... I remember I was at this
> weekend seminar at Princeton once — and
> there was this one speaker ... Henry Sa
> ... Henry ... uh ... Henry ...

He stops, as if his memory escaped without any warning.

> PARRY
> (continuing)
> ... What was I saying?

JACK is as surprised as he is. PARRY's face is frightened
and confused again. There is panic in his voice.

> PARRY
> (continuing)
> ... What was I saying?

He raises his head to look and sees:

53   **EXT.   SHEEPS MEADOW — SEVERAL YARDS AWAY — NIGHT**

THE DARK SILHOUETTE OF THE RED KNIGHT UPON HIS HORSE.
Staring — knowing exactly where PARRY lies even though it's
dark.

PARRY looks frightened as he lays his head back down. JACK
tries to snap him out of it by saying:

> JACK
> How come you've never asked that girl
> for a date?

PARRY looks back to see that the RED KNIGHT has vanished. He

(CONTINUED)

starts to snap out of it somewhat.

                PARRY
I can't ask for her ... I have to earn
her.

                JACK
Parry, you don't have to earn a woman.
It's the twentieth century.

                PARRY
Maybe, when we get the Grail ...

                JACK
Well, see, I think she can help ... You
know how women are great ... they ...
they make homes and they ... ya know,
kill the livestock so the knights can go
out and get Grails and ... slaughter vil-
lages with a clear head ... I mean, where
would Arthur be without Guinevere ...

                PARRY
Happily married, probably.

                JACK
Bad example. Just trust me. A woman who
loves you keeps you going ... gives you
strength ... makes you feel like you can
do anything ...

                PARRY
Is that what your girlfriend does for
you?

                JACK
       (hesitates; then lies)
Sure ...

                                CUT TO:

55   INT.   LOBBY, MET LIFE BUILDING — MORNING

JACK waits near the elevators as the nine-to-five crowd
makes its way into the building. He looks like a bum —
having stayed out all night with PARRY. He's so tired he
can't keep his eyes open as LYDIA walks with the crowd to
the elevator. Just as the doors close, JACK spots her and
jumps in between them — causing the inhabitants a jolt.

                                CUT TO:

56   INT.   TWO HEARTS PUBLISHING — MORNING

The elevator doors open. LYDIA gets off after two leggy
BUSINESSWOMEN. JACK follows. She walks through two glass

                             (CONTINUED)

doors with the words Two Hearts Publishing, Inc. and enters
the office. JACK waits until she has disappeared down a
foyer, then enters the reception area.

                    JACK
          Could you help me — what was the name of
          that girl who just came in?

                    RECEPTIONIST
          What girl? I didn't notice.

                    JACK
          Uh ... she was wearing a kind of ... a
          flouncy kind of ... uh ... plain ...

He makes big gestures with his arms to describe the dress,
the stringy gestures with his fingers to describe her hair.

                    RECEPTIONIST
               (winning at charades)
          Oh, Lydia!

                    JACK
          Lydia. Lydia what?

                    RECEPTIONIST
          God, I have no idea. She's worked here
          for fifteen years and I have no idea.
          I'll call her.

                    JACK
          No ... no ... that's all right ... I
          thought I knew her ... Thanks ...

                                                    CUT TO:

58   INT.   **VIDEO SPOT OFFICE — DAY**

JACK is on the phone, with an open Yellow Pages beside him.

                    JACK
          Yes. Two Hearts Publishing? May I speak
          to Lydia please.

He waits. ANNE enters. She is obviously very irritated with
him.

                    ANNE
          Can I have my desk please.

                    JACK
               (to phone)
          Hello, I'd like to speak to Lydia?

                    ANNE
          Lydia?! Lydia who!?

                                              (CONTINUED)

                    JACK
              (to ANNE)
    I don't know her last name ... I'll be
    off in a second.

                    ANNE
    You're calling *Lydia* in *my* office. You
    must think I'm some dope. You fuckin'
    bastard ... You ...
              (she punches his arm)
    ... stay out all night long ...

                    JACK
              (overlapping, to phone)
    What ... No ... Lydia ... I want to
    speak to ... her name is Lydia ... I ...
    uh ...

                    ANNE
              (overlapping)
    ... I don't get a friggin' phone call.
    You stroll in here at noon. I got ...
    two people out sick. Ya think I need
    this? I DO NOT NEED THIS!

                    JACK
    ... *Forget it ... goodbye!*

He hangs up.

ANNE sits down at her desk. She is waiting for an
explanation.

                    JACK
              (continuing)
    I was not out with a woman last night. I
    was out with Parry.

                    ANNE
    The moron?

                    JACK
    He's not a moron.

                    ANNE
    And who's Lydia?

                    JACK
    Lydia is the girl Parry likes ... and I
    thought, if I could get them together
    I ...

                    ANNE
    What? The curse'll be lifted? *Will you
    please!*

                                        (CONTINUED)

> JACK
> I ... You're not going to understand
> this.

> ANNE
> Don't treat me like I'm stupid. It
> pisses me off.

> JACK
> All right ... Sorry ... I feel indebted
> to him.

> ANNE
> (pause)
> What does that mean?

> JACK
> See, I told you!

> ANNE
> Well, what the hell does that mean?

> JACK
> I thought ... if ... if I can help him
> in some way ... you know? ... get him
> this girl he loves ... then ... maybe
> ... things'll start changing for me ...
> My luck, ya know ... Maybe ...
> (gives up)
> Forget it ... It's a stupid idea.

ANNE looks at him incredulously. He sits down and breathes a sigh — the absurdity of the idea hitting him as well. ANNE softens — feeling like she has unfairly taken the wind out of his sail.

> ANNE
> Oh, you poor kid ... You're a mess.

ANNE stands and buries JACK's face in her breast. She decides to be positive.

> ANNE
> (continuing)
> ... Well, listen ... stranger things
> have happened.

CUT TO:

A59   INT.   ANNE'S APARTMENT — LATER THAT AFTERNOON

JACK on the phone to LYDIA. This time ANNE is right beside him.

> JACK
> Hello, Lydia?

(CONTINUED)

> LYDIA
> (abrasively)
> Yeah? Who is this?

Her abrupt manner surprises JACK. JACK uses his old,
confident radio voice.

> JACK
> This is Jack Lucas and I'm calling from
> Video Spot video rentals.

59   INT.   LYDIA'S OFFICE — INTERCUT PHONE CALL — DAY

> LYDIA
> Yes.

> JACK
> Yes, well ...
> (guessing and hoping)
> You are a credit card holder, are you
> not?

> LYDIA
> Uh-huh.

> JACK
> Well, congratulations, Lydia, because
> out of several thousand card holders ...
> in conjunction with several major credit
> card companies ...

> LYDIA
> Which ones?

> JACK
> All of them ... Which means *you* have
> just won a free membership at our store
> on Second Avenue.

He puts the receiver near a tape player and presses play.
"Happy Days Are Here Again" plays for a moment, then he
shuts it off.

> LYDIA
> How did this happen?

JACK is prepared for LYDIA's, shall we say, reluctance to
buy it!

> JACK
> Your name was picked.

> LYDIA
> (suspicious ... and dense)
> Well, I don't understand. What did you
> do — did you pick my name out of a hat
> or ... or ... a list?

(CONTINUED)

71

                    JACK
          A list.

                    LYDIA
          Well — were there a lot of people in the
          room or just you or what?

                    JACK
          Well there was ...
                    (then)
          What's the difference?

                    LYDIA
          Well, I mean ... I don't know you ...
          This has never ... I've never won
          anything and ... I don't have a VCR.

                    JACK
          You get a VCR with the membership.
                    (ANNE hits him)
          ... for a short time until you get your
          own. Listen, why don't you come down to
          the store and you can check it out. See
          if you're interested.

                    LYDIA
          Did Phyllis in accounting tell you to
          call me?

                    JACK
                    (fed up)
          No! I told you! You won a contest!

LYDIA hangs up. JACK turns to ANNE.

                    JACK
          ... This is going to be rough.

                                                  CUT TO:

59A   INT.   MET LIFE ELEVATOR — DAY

JACK stands beside a costumed GAY BUM in a crowded elevator.
The BUM warms up to the elevator's Muzak. JACK shoves him to
stop.

A somber-looking BUSINESSMAN rides alongside, reading a
newspaper. The GAY BUM moves next to him and looks up.

                    GAY BUM
          I'm Anne Morrow Lindbergh and I can't
          find my baby ...

The BUSINESSMAN is stunned. He laughs.

                    BUSINESSMAN
          What?

                                              (CONTINUED)

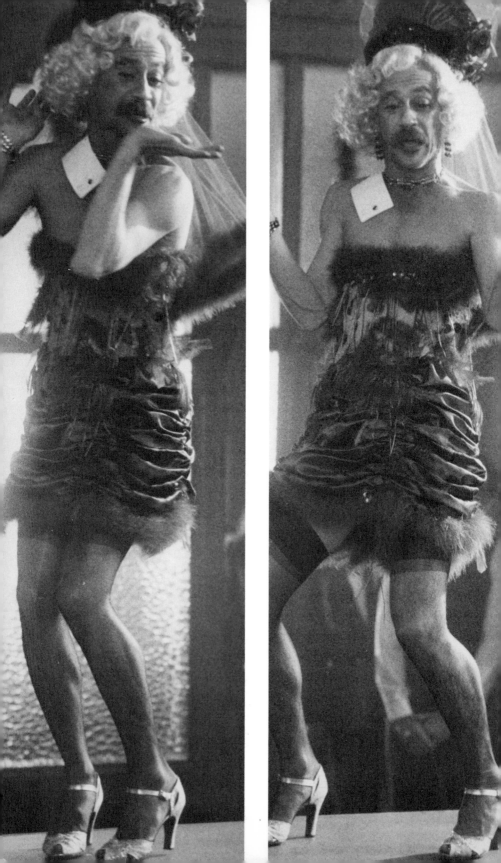

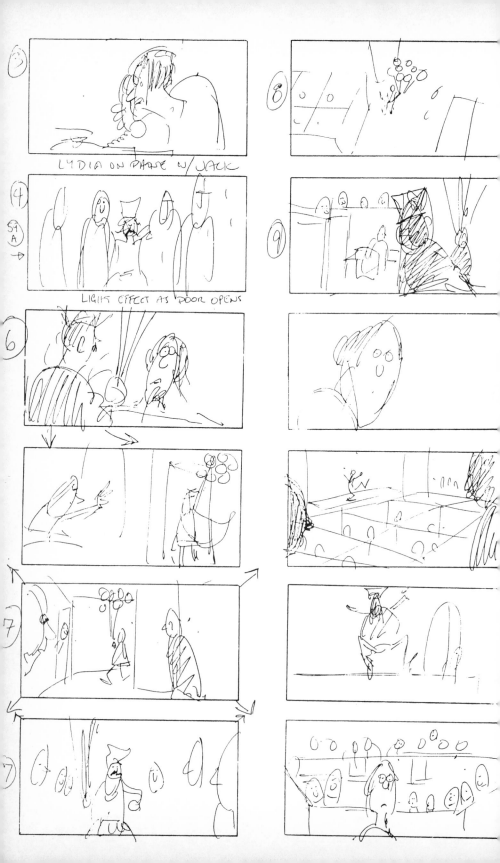

LYDIA ON DANSE W/ JACK

LIGHT EFFECT AS DOOR OPENS

> GAY BUM
> See, I knew I could make you smile ...

                                          CUT TO:

60   INT.   TWO HEARTS PUBLISHING — DAY

The elevator doors open. JACK stands beside the GAY BUM who carries balloons marked VIDEO SPOT.

> JACK
> (adamant)
> Remember. One chorus and out.

> GAY BUM
> I'm a man with a misson, Jack.

The GAY BUM walks to the office entrance. JACK pushes the down button. As the doors close, we hear him say to himself:

> JACK
> I can't believe I'm on a first name basis with these people ...

The GAY BUM enters the reception area, much to the surprise of the receptionist.

> RECEPTIONIST
> Can I ... help you?

> GAY BUM
> Is there a mousy woman who works here named Lydia?

> RECEPTIONIST
> Yes ... if you'll wait here I'll ...

> GAY BUM
> This is a personalized message. I have to give it in person.

61   INT.   TWO HEARTS PUBLISHING — MOMENTS LATER

The GAY BUM strolls nonchalantly into the office and down the aisle relishing the amazed expressions of the employees. He approaches a cubicle on which he reads a small nameplate — LYDIA SINCLAIR. LYDIA has her back to him, but slowly turns as she feels someone watching her. She lets out a tiny scream when she sees him standing there like a deranged clown. The GAY BUM takes notice of her outfit — a corduroy, forest green jumper with a lime green turtleneck.

> GAY BUM
> You MUST be SHE.

                                          (CONTINUED)

61   CONTINUED:

                         LYDIA
            Huh?

The GAY BUM begins to sing a song parody to the tune of a
classical musical number (song to be chosen). After a big
finish, the GAY BUM hands LYDIA a business card, drops the
act and exits.

                         GAY BUM
                  (murmurs cynically)
            Jesus ...

Stunned, LYDIA looks down at the information card she holds
frozen in her hand.

                                            CUT TO:

62   **INT. VIDEO SPOT — LATER**

C.U. on ANNE, who is slightly repulsed by PARRY.

PARRY, his hair slicked back, wearing a Video Spot T-shirt
over his clothes. JACK hangs a pine car freshener around
PARRY's neck to help with the smell. The bell in the front
door jingles.

LYDIA cautiously enters the store.

Behind the counter, JACK spots her immediately and nudges
ANNE. She turns to look. Her bra straps are visible. JACK
fixes them.

                         LYDIA
            Hello. My name is Lydia Sinclair.

                         JACK
            Yes. Hi ... Congratulations. Jack Lucas.
            Nice to meet you finally. This is Anne
            Napolitano, owner of Video Spot.

                         ANNE
            Hello ... congratulations.

                         JACK
            And this is our ... uh ... co-worker ...
            Parry ... uh ... Parry ...

                         LYDIA
            Parry Parry?

                         PARRY
            No, just Parry.

                         LYDIA
            Oh ... like Moses.

                                         (CONTINUED)

74

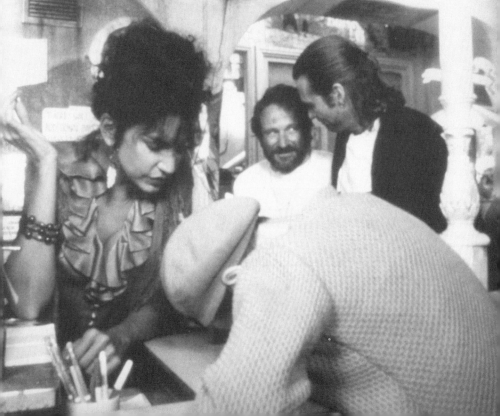

No one knows how to respond to this, so they don't.

                    LYDIA
              (continuing; curt)
      So how do we do this?!

                    JACK
      Well ... um ... you get an official
      membership card ...
              (takes one out)
      Just sign that and we'll laminate it
      right here ... Parry? You want to
      laminate Miss Sinclair's card? ...

PARRY stands staring at her.

                    JACK
              (continuing)
      ... Parry?

PARRY snaps out of it and crosses from behind the counter to
the laminating machine next to JACK.

                    ANNE
      This will last you one year after which
      you have the option to renew if ... you
      like at a membership discount.

                    LYDIA
              (defensive)
      But now it's free, right?

                    ANNE
      Yeah.

ANNE backs off. She stands next to an equally perplexed JACK
as they watch LYDIA fill out the card. Her abrasive demeanor
is not what they expected. LYDIA finishes the card and
pushes it toward them.

                    JACK
      Uh ... you ... you can pick out up to
      ten movies ...

                    LYDIA
      Free?

                    JACK
      Yes. They're free.

                    ANNE
              (butts in)
      Only the first ten. After that they're
      2.99 a rental.

LYDIA eyes ANNE suspiciously, then turns to survey the

                                 (CONTINUED)

shelves. PARRY picks up her card and laminates it — all the
while keeping his eyes fixed upon LYDIA's every move. ANNE
and JACK, having set the trap, watch with interest.

LYDIA surveys the film boxes, H-L. She spots one of interest
and pulls it off the shelf — causing two other boxes to fall
down on her. She catches one box and, as she replaces it
back on the shelf, causes three more to fall. She catches
two of the three.

PARRY, ANNE and JACK watch with an odd fascination. JACK
nudges PARRY to forget the laminating and go help her. PARRY
gathers up his nerve and moves from around the counter, up
behind her.

> PARRY
> ... Can ... can I help you?

LYDIA quickly turns — she is uncomfortable by his closeness.

> LYDIA
> No. No ... I can look myself ...

She moves away abruptly — like a fox terrier who pretends to
ignore the mess she made on the living room rug.

PARRY turns to JACK and ANNE, as if to say "What do I do
now?" JACK encourages him to keep trying. PARRY organizes
the boxes and picks one out.

> PARRY
> How about *Hell Merchants*?

> LYDIA
> I don't like horror movies!

> PARRY
> How about ... Zbiegnew Speizak's *The
> Purple Bread*, an intensely portrayed
> tale of love and envy set against the
> sweeping background of a Polish bakery.
> In subtitles.

> LYDIA
> I don't like ... uh ...
> (finding it hard to categorize)
> Polish love stories ...
> (she turns her back on him, but
> adds)
> ... I like musicals.

> PARRY
> (encouraged)
> Well, we have plenty of those. Right
> over here. We got the MGM series,
> Astaire and Rogers, the Judy
> Garlands ...

(CONTINUED)

                         LYDIA
               Got any Ethel Merman?

He doesn't see any. He looks to ANNE, who shakes her head.

                         PARRY
               ... Uh ... we seem to be all out of
               Ethel Merman.

                         LYDIA
               What a gyp.

                         PARRY
               Yeah.

Pause. JACK nudges ANNE to do something.

                         ANNE
               You know, I think I ... ordered some
               just the other day.

                         LYDIA
               Well did you or didn't you?

                         ANNE
                    (pissed off)
               Yes! They'll be in soon.

                         LYDIA
               Well, I guess I'll come back then.

                         JACK
               Here's your card.

LYDIA walks back to the counter. As JACK hands her the card,
she notices ANNE's painted star fingernails.

                         LYDIA
               I like your nails. where did you get
               them done?

                         ANNE
               Ah ... I do them myself. I used to work
               in a beauty parlor.

LYDIA keeps staring at them. She says blankly:

                         LYDIA
               I like the stars.

JACK gets an idea.

                         JACK
               You know, Anne does other people too.
               Sort of a sideline ...
                    (ANNE is surprised to hear this)
               ... If you want, she could do your
               nails.

                                        (CONTINUED)

LYDIA
How much?

JACK
Well, since you're a member, we
could ...

ANNE
(interrupts)
Twenty dollars.

LYDIA considers the offer. PARRY waits for the outcome.

LYDIA
Okay ... twenty dollars ... When can
you ...

JACK
Tonight! How's tonight?

LYDIA thinks. ANNE is ready to kill JACK. PARRY smiles
hopefully.

CUT TO:

63   INT.   ANNE'S APARTMENT — THAT EVENING

JACK searches frantically through a closet. ANNE and PARRY
sit opposite each other at the table. PARRY is eating ANNE's
home cooking voraciously. ANNE doesn't quite know how to
take PARRY, who smiles mischieviously through his meal.

ANNE
(to JACK O.S.)
Getting your nails done is one thing but
going to dinner with a bunch of
strangers and *him* ... She didn't even
look at him.

PARRY
Got any more bread crust?

As ANNE resentfully rises and crosses into the kitchen,
PARRY focuses on her robust breasts bouncing beneath the
sweater. ANNE's expression, as she serves him, is a mixture
of repulsion and fascination. She sits at the table.

JACK (O.S.)
We'll make it very casual ... not like
having a date or anything. I just have
to find something he'll look good in.

ANNE looks at PARRY as if this were an impossibility. PARRY
smiles back — he likes ANNE.

(CONTINUED)

                    ANNE
        I don't know ... He's a little
        disgusting ... Although some women go
        for that.

                    JACK (O.S.)
        He just needs some clothes.

                    PARRY
        Got any more starchy food?

Another opportunity to watch ANNE's breasts in action, as
she reluctantly rises to get him more macaroni. She returns
with the pot.

                    ANNE
        I mean, I've gone out with bums, but
        they were gorgeous. It's the only reason
        to go out with a bum.

                    PARRY
        This food's delicious. You're a
        wonderful cook. And you have a lovely
        home.

                    ANNE
        Jack, he's starting a conversation ...

                    JACK (O.S.)
        Well, talk back. He won't bite you.

                    ANNE
              (cool and polite)
        Thank you very much.

                    PARRY
              (enjoying the conversation)
        You're welcome. You know, a beautiful
        woman like yourself — your own business
        — I'm surprised some guy doesn't snatch
        you up for his own.

ANNE looks in JACK's direction, but replies to PARRY:

                    ANNE
        You're surprised! ... But I guess I just
        never met the right guy. Whatta gonna
        do?

                    PARRY
        I'm shocked. With a child bearing body
        like yours ...
              (ANNE doesn't know how to take
               that)
        ... why a man would have to be out of
        his mind!

                                        (CONTINUED)

> ANNE
> Most men are.

> PARRY
> Why, this is outrageous!

PARRY, getting overly heated, slams down his fork. ANNE jumps.

> PARRY
> (continuing)
> ... A woman of your value going to waste
> before my eyes ...
> (rising intensity)
> Come on! I'm yours! Let's go!
> (clears the table with one move)
> Come on — let us go to that place of
> splendor in the grass.

He starts to unzip his pants.

> ANNE
> *Jack!*

Climbing over the table to her, he serenades.

> PARRY
> Holdin' my penis ...
> What a lovely way of sayin' how
> Much ya like me ...

> ANNE
> *What are you, out of your mind?*

JACK enters.

> PARRY
> Holdin' my penis ...

> JACK
> *Parry!* Close your pants ...

PARRY stops singing and gets off the table. He bows to her.

> PARRY
> (kidding)
> You sure now?

ANNE looks at him like she's going to belt him.

> PARRY
> (continuing)
> ... Well, alright. But you let me know.
> (with great sincerity)
> You're too good a woman to go to waste.

(CONTINUED)

63   CONTINUED:

ANNE, in spite of herself, agrees with him. She looks to
JACK to see if he agrees, but JACK is too busy inspecting
PARRY.

                    JACK
          What are you — a 40 in a jacket?

ANNE, frustrated with the two of them, exits.

63A   **EXT.   VIDEO SPOT — NIGHT**

LYDIA walks up and RINGS the bell. Buzzed in, she enters.

                                              CUT TO:

64   **INT.   ANNE'S APARTMENT — LATER THAT EVENING**

ANNE opens the door to a cautious LYDIA. LYDIA nods,
self-consciously, as if to say, "Yeah, I'm here."

                    ANNE
          Hello ... welcome ... come in.

LYDIA enters, subtly inspecting the apartment.

                    LYDIA
          I've never been in an apartment above a
          store. You always pass them on the
          street but you never think anyone really
          lives in them.

                    ANNE
               (raising an eyebrow)
          Can I get you anything ... coffee ...
          tea ... a little tequila?

                    LYDIA
          No, thank you.

LYDIA sits at the formica table, already set up with nail
care paraphernalia — with the gleaming steel nail files it
looks a bit like surgery equipment.

                    LYDIA
          Will it hurt?

                    ANNE
               (threateningly)
          That all depends on you. ... Sure you
          don't want a drink?

LYDIA's a little bit nervous about this attempt at nail
beauty.

81

64A INT. PARRY'S BASEMENT — NIGHT

JACK is cleaning up PARRY — perhaps applying a green mud
treatment.

CUT TO:

65 INT. ANNE'S APARTMENT — LATER THAT EVENING

ANNE is seated at her formica table opposite LYDIA. She
delicately holds one of LYDIA's hands, carefully applying
the stars to her nails. LYDIA sips her tequila with one
hand. ANNE's glass is almost empty as she talks nonstop:

                    ANNE
          ... So he says to me, "You'll never find
          another man like me."... I said,
          "Please, men like you have one hand on
          their dicks and the other hand on their
          mother's leg ... I said, there's the
          door — take a trip."

                    LYDIA
               (paying close attention)
          You threw him out?

ANNE makes a confident nod. LYDIA sips.

                    LYDIA
          My parents were divorced.

                    ANNE
          It's an awful thing, let me tell you. My
          aunt used to say,
               (emphasizing)
          "Divorce is the sister-in-law of death."

ANNE nods knowingly. LYDIA squints as she considers this.

CUT TO:

66 INT. PARRY'S BASEMENT — SAME TIME

JACK stands behind a seated PARRY in front of a mirror.
PARRY's hair is wet. JACK places a can of styling mousse in
front of him. PARRY squeezes a ball of mousse in his hand,
then applies it to his head. PARRY proceeds to experiment
with a number of styles — adding more and more mousse as
JACK watches in silence. PARRY molds his hair into a cone,
then divides into two cones, then mushes it into a
pompadour, then splits the pompadour — PARRY is having a
wonderful time — applying enormous amounts to his head and
eyebrows. Finally, JACK grabs the can out of PARRY's hand.

67   INT.   **ANNE'S APARTMENT — A LITTLE LATER**

ANNE works on LYDIA's other hand, as LYDIA sips her tequila
from a straw.

                    ANNE
          ... So ... anybody special in your life?

                    LYDIA
               (defensive)
          Do I look like I have someone special?

She moves to pick up her tequila with the manicured hand but
ANNE eyes her down.

                    ANNE
          Well, don't say it like that. It's not
          so ... ya know, crazy an idea. You are a
          healthy woman ... you hold a steady job.
          Ya not cross-eyed or anything ...

                    LYDIA
          Well, there's nobody special!

                    ANNE
          Fine.

                    LYDIA
               (pause, then:)
          I mean, it's not easy in this day and
          age.

                    ANNE
          What?

                    LYDIA
          Meeting ... people.

                    ANNE
          Tell me about it. I've been dating
          longer than I've been driving. I can't
          believe that.

                    LYDIA
          I never really ... went through a ...
          dating period.

                    ANNE
          It's a disgusting process. You haven't
          missed anything.

LYDIA nods in agreement, but her face tells us she feels she
has missed a great deal.

68   INT.   PARRY'S BASEMENT — NIGHT

PARRY, cleaned and dressed up — his hair moussed back, the
suit is too big. PARRY paces back and forth in the hallway
as JACK tries to staple the sleeves of the suit shorter for
PARRY's arms.

                    JACK
          Will you stand still so I can do this!

                    PARRY
          I'm sorry ... I'm just so excited.
               (JACK smiles)
          You must have felt this way when you
          first met Anne, huh? where did you two
          meet?

                    JACK
          In a bar called Hellfire.

                    PARRY
          Tch ... how romantic. Yeah. If I wasn't
          already committed to Lydia, boy. Except
          Anne'd never go for me though. She loves
          you too much. And you really love her,
          huh?

                    JACK
          No. But that's not the only reason
          people get together or ... stay
          together.

                    PARRY
          What are the other reasons?

JACK thinks a moment, then answers plainly:

                    JACK
          Survival.

PARRY puts his arm on JACK's shoulder and speaks very
sincerely.

                    PARRY
               (earnest)
          You love her a lot, Jack. You're ...
          crazy about her ... It's just that,
          sometimes, you're a little bit of an
          asshole.

JACK is surprised by the remark and abruptly focuses on
PARRY.

69 INT.   ANNE'S APARTMENT — LATER

LYDIA is a little more loose and talkative now as ANNE
refills her glass, then takes LYDIA's other hand to apply
the stars.

                    LYDIA
                (deadpan)
          ... My mother calls every week. Like a
          recurring nightmare. "So, have you met
          anyone?" ... "No, Mom." ... "So what's
          going to happen?" ... "I don't know,
          Mom." ... I only thank God I moved out.

                    ANNE
          I can't believe you lived with her that
          long. If I had to live with my mother,
          I'd stab myself six times.

                    LYDIA
          I think some people are meant to be
          alone.
                (she takes a slug)
          Maybe I was a man in a former life and I
          used women for pleasure so now I'm
          paying for it — which would be fine, if
          I could just remember some of the
          pleasure parts ...
                (drinks)

                    ANNE
          I don't understand you. What is the
          problem?

                    LYDIA
          I don't feel like I make any impression
          on people ... At office parties I spend
          my time re-arranging the hors d'oeuvres
          as people eat them, so the platters will
          always look full. I don't start conversa-
          tions because I have no idea how to end
          them ... I think I'm just meant to live
          in the background of things ...

                    ANNE
          That's not true ... You gotta ease up
          ... Conversations have a life of their
          own. You gotta just go with it ... We're
          having a lovely conversation.

                    LYDIA
                (bluntly)
          I'm paying you.

ANNE drops her hand. She's pissed.

                                        (CONTINUED)

>   ANNE
> You know, let me tell you something! I'm
> not that kind of person. I don't do
> people favors. If I talk to you it's
> because I want to. So we're not all ...
> uh ... Jerri Hall ... Big Deal ... What
> a boring world if we were. You do the
> best you can with what you got. You're
> not invisible, ya know ... You want to
> make an impression? Try this: you can be
> a real bitch.

>   LYDIA
>   (her face lights up)
> Really?

>   ANNE
> Yeah!

LYDIA smiles at the thought of having such an impressionable
personality.

69A   EXT.   VIDEO SPOT — NIGHT

JACK tries to calm PARRY down.

>   JACK
> Come here ... you're all crooked.
>   (hands him wallet)
> Here's my wallet, so you can pay for
> dinner.

JACK adjusts PARRY's tie, then undoes it and re-ties. PARRY
take the wallet, kepping his eyes on JACK, as JACK primps
him.

>   PARRY
> ... You're a nice man, Jack. Doing all
> this for me ...

JACK doesn't pay attention as PARRY's expression grows pale
and frightened. He suddenly wraps his arms around JACK and
whispers:

>   PARRY
> I'm scared, Jack.

JACK, uncomfortable at the intimacy, tries to comfort him.

>   PARRY
> ... I feel so much for her ... I feel
> like something awful is going to happen.

                                               (CONTINUED)

                          JACK
          No. Nothing bad's going to happen.
          Anne'll be there. I'll be there. Nothing
          bad will happen.

                          PARRY
          I'm still scared.

                                          CUT BACK TO:

69B   INT.   **ANNE'S APARTMENT — NIGHT**

ANNE and LYDIA share a drink.

                          ANNE
          It's hard being a woman. I don't care
          what anybody says ... People say we have
          choices — we have *no* choices ... My
          grandma used to say that for a woman, in
          this world behind every door there's
          either death ... or husband.

LYDIA cracks up laughing.

                          LYDIA
          "Sister-in-law of death" ... That's
          wonderful.

She takes another sip as JACK knocks on the door and enters
with PARRY.

                          JACK
          Anne ... !
                   (to LYDIA)
          Oh, hi. How's it going?

LYDIA loses her smile and becomes self-conscious and
protective.

                          JACK
          Parry, it's Lydia Sinclair — our
          membership winner.

                          PARRY
          I know!

JACK turns to find that PARRY is still outside the
apartment. He crosses to PARRY. The two whisper intensely.

                          ANNE
          What are you two up to?

                          JACK
          Well ... everything's closed up. We
          thought we'd get some dinner.
                   (overplaying it)
                   (MORE)

                                          (CONTINUED)

87

                              JACK (CONTINUED)
              Say! ... anybody for Chinese?
                    (to LYDIA)
              Have you eaten? Would you like to come
              along?

                              LYDIA
                    (rises, uncomfortable)
              Oh, no ... I have to get home ...

                              ANNE
              The nails!! Watch the nails!! ...
                    (LYDIA sits back down)
              Listen, you still have to eat.

PARRY stands in B.G. with JACK, whispering.

                              LYDIA
              No, really ... I can't.

                              ANNE
              Hey. What did I tell you? Why don't you
              come? It's just dinner. You'll have
              something to tell your mother next time
              she calls.

LYDIA smiles as PARRY and JACK reach an agreement. All four
turn to each other spontaneously and say:

                         ANNE, JACK, LYDIA, PARRY
              Fine.

                                                      CUT TO:

70A EXT.   **STREET NEAR BROOKLYN BRIDGE — NIGHT**

PARRY and LYDIA walk and talk. ANNE and JACK walk behind
them.

                              LYDIA
              ... I ... uh ... I get to read some of
              the books but mostly I ... just
              calculate production costs from first
              edition hard cover publication to
              paperback. After paperback it's
              basically someone else's problem.

                              PARRY
              It sounds exciting.

                              LYDIA
              Why does it sound exciting? there's
              absolutely nothing exciting about it.

As PARRY talks, he picks up a piece of garbage on the
sidewalk.

                                                 (CONTINUED)

> PARRY
> Well, you're calculating costs that
> could have an effect on whether or not
> the book is published and if it is, it
> could be a book that ... might somehow
> change the way people think or act — a
> book can do that. And you would be part
> of creating a cultural shift that could
> change our society forever.

PARRY deposits the garbage in a garbage can and is almost
about to browse through it when:

> JACK
> Parry!

PARRY is alerted by JACK that this would be inappropriate.
However, he does take a wire champagne cork wrapper,
discreetly.

> LYDIA
> We mostly publish trashy romance novels.

> PARRY
> Well — empires have fallen because of
> trashy romances ...

PARRY seems to be fashioning something out of the wire.

> PARRY
> (continuing)
> ... Romance is romance no matter what
> kind it is ... It could be a Victorian
> lady kidnapped by a virile sea captain
> with a hairy chest ... or a horny pizza
> boy seduced by a housewife with a hairy
> upper lip. As long as there's heart,
> passion, and a little bit of fantasy ...
> romance is the stuff of dreams ...
> there's always more to trash than meets
> the eye ...

With this, PARRY shows her his creation — a little wire
chair made from the champagne wire. LYDIA is impressed.
Their eyes meet for a dangerous moment, until:

A LARGE MAN walks by, bumping into LYDIA without apology and
knocking PARRY's gift to the ground.

> PARRY
> Hey!

The LARGE MAN continues walking as PARRY reaches to his back
pocket to pull out his slingshot when:

> JACK, ANNE
> PARRY!

(CONTINUED)

89

PARRY begrudgingly lets him go.

> MARTIN (O.S.)
> Parry! ... Parry — is that you?

PARRY spots a familiar homeless face, sitting on the curb.

> PARRY
> Hey Martin ...!

> MARTIN
> Don't you look all duded up!

> PARRY
> This is Lydia!

> MARTIN
> Nice to meet you Lydia! Got a quarter?!

PARRY smiles proudly. A mortified LYDIA reaches in her purse and hands MARTIN a quarter. ANNE and JACK watch in disbelief.

> MARTIN
> Thank you. God bless ...
> (To PARRY)
> Nice girl ... Have you set the date yet?

LYDIA hurries away. PARRY follows. The walk continues.

> LYDIA
> How do you know him?

> PARRY
> We were neighbors for a couple of weeks
> on Sutton Place.

> LYDIA
> You lived on Sutton Place?

> PARRY
> (proudly)
> Yep! Right on it!

> ANNE
> (tries to save it)
> Huh ... the restaurant's just around the
> corner here ...

They nod. After a beat, LYDIA asks:

> LYDIA
> What do you do — for a living, I mean?

> PARRY
> Well, I'm in search of the Holy Grail.

(CONTINUED)

JACK smacks his own forehead, exasperated. ANNE gives up.

                                                    CUT TO:

71   **INT.   CHINESE RESTAURANT — NIGHT**

ANNE and LYDIA sit opposite JACK and PARRY. They are served
three large orders of dumplings.

                         ANNE
          Oh ... I could eat all of these.

LYDIA is nervous about this. As everyone begins to eat, she
eyes her chopsticks with reluctance.

PARRY looks at her and smiles encouragingly. LYDIA forces a
smile back, picks up her chopsticks and dives in. PARRY
watches her in adoration. JACK subtly tries to get PARRY to
stop staring. But PARRY is glued to his vision.

LYDIA, even more awkward now with her new nails, drops her
first dumpling into her lap.

                         LYDIA
          Oh ... God ...

To save her from embarrassment, PARRY drops his dumpling
into his lap as well.

                         PARRY
          Oh boy ...

LYDIA takes her napkin and dips it into a glass of water.
PARRY follows suit.

When LYDIA removes the napkin, her glass falls over. PARRY
forces his glass over as well.

ANNE and JACK are looking at this mirror exercise in
fascination.

                         PARRY
                      (to LYDIA)
          Can't take us anywhere, huh?

LYDIA can't help but smile — a little more at ease now,
grateful she is not the clumsy center of attention.

JACK leans over and whispers to ANNE:

                         JACK
          What do you think?

                         ANNE
          I think they're made for each other. And
          it scares me.

                                              (CONTINUED)

FADE TO:

LATER IN THE EVENING. WE PAN the table as everyone eats their main courses.

LYDIA, we discover, has another eating idiosyncrasy. She unconsiously, but quite loudly, smacks her mouth when she chews.

> LYDIA (O.C.)
> SMACK ... SMACK ... SMACK ...

We hear this smacking off camera as we begin on JACK, trying not to look at LYDIA but having difficulty enjoying his own meal. CAMERA moves to PARRY, staring at her, helplessly in love, not paying any attention to his own food; moving to LYDIA "smack, smacking," beginning to accept PARRY's attraction in her and, warming up to the idea, she throws a smile at him between "smacks"; and finally ANNE, chewing quietly, staring at JACK with her eyes widened twice their normal size, indicating her disbelief at LYDIA's vocal variety of noises.

CUT TO:

PARRY, gazing at his sweetheart, a song to serenade comes to mind and he softly begins:

> PARRY
> Lydia ... Oh Lydia ... That
> encyclopedia. Oh Lydia the tattooed lady
> ...

His gentle voice counterbalances the odd lyrics and makes it sound like a love song.

ANNE eyes JACK to stop him.

JACK is about to make an attempt but can't seem to find the way, so he doesn't bother.

LYDIA doesn't know how to respond either. At first she smiles politely, then she pretends to be too busy eating to listen — but something about PARRY's sincerity pulls her in. His face glows as he floats the lyrics across the table to her. Slowly, her smacking subsides, she lowers her fork, forgets her self-consciousness and listens to PARRY — slightly hypnotized, like a little girl watching a ballerina for the first time.

JACK is fascinated by PARRY's complete adoration of this complete mess of a woman. He looks to ANNE, who tries to continue her meal nonchalantly. He notices her bra strap hanging out from her sweater.

CAMERA CUTS BACK AND FORTH between the exposed strap and

(CONTINUED)

JACK, as PARRY continues serenading O.S. ANNE realizes JACK
is staring at her and immediately thinks something is wrong.
But JACK just smiles at her. His hand reaches across the
table, not to fix her sweater, but to take her hand. ANNE is
in shock. She slips her hand into his and smiles back, her
eyes almost tearing.

When PARRY finishes, he smiles.

> PARRY
> Would it be all right ... I mean would
> you mind ... if I walked you home
> tonight?

LYDIA nods. From O.S., PARRY's hand holds a napkin and
gently dabs a stain of soy sauce on her sleeve.

                                                    CUT TO:

72   EXT.   VIDEO SPOT — NIGHT

ANNE and JACK are walking home from the Chinese restaurant.

> ANNE
> I think she went for him. I can't
> believe it.

> JACK
> I know, I know. I really did it.

> ANNE
> Omnia Vincit Amor!

> JACK
> What?

> ANNE
> Omnia Vincit Amor!
> (haughtily)
> It's Latin. It means "Love Conquers
> All."

She notices Jack looking at her skeptically.

> ANNE
> (continuing)
> I don't mean us, I don't mean us. I mean
> everybody else.

> JACK
> Do you really think it will work out?

> ANNE
> (unlocking street door)
> Who knows? Two people can be at a party
> and never find each other. Another two
>   (MORE)

                                              (CONTINUED)

93

> ANNE (CONTINUED)
> people could be on opposite sides of the
> world and nothing can keep them apart.
> The thing is, if a thing is meant to
> happen ...

She becomes self-conscious, noticing that JACK is staring at
her.

> ANNE
> (continuing)
> What? What's the matter?

> JACK
> Nothing.

JACK moves to enter the building when ANNE stops him.

> ANNE
> Well ... I think you should feel very
> proud. You did a real nice thing for
> somebody else. I'm very proud.

> JACK
> You were great. Thanks a lot.

He kisses her hard and long. ANNE pulls away to catch her
breath. She is surprised, to say the least.

> ANNE
> You're welcome.

JACK tenderly brushes her hair off her face. He kisses her
again.

> ANNE
> Oh my.

CUT TO:

73   **EXT.   LYDIA'S STREET — NIGHT**

PARRY and LYDIA walk — noticeably more comfortable with each
other than before.

> PARRY
> Tell me more. I want to know everything.

> LYDIA
> There isn't any more to tell.

> PARRY
> Don't say that.

> LYDIA
> (genuine)
> No, really ... believe me — there isn't
> any more. This is it.

(CONTINUED)

                    PARRY
          Well, it's enough for me.

                    LYDIA
          You don't have to say that.

                    PARRY
          I never say anything I have to.

                    LYDIA
          I mean you don't have to say nice things
          to me ... That kind of thing is a little
          old fashioned for what we're about to
          do.

                    PARRY
          What are we about to do?

                    LYDIA
          Well ... you're walking me home. I ... I
          guess you're sort of ... attracted to me
          and you'll want to come upstairs for ...
          coffee ...

                    PARRY
          I don't drink coffee ...

                    LYDIA
          ... and then we'll probably have a drink
          and get comfortable with each other and
          ... and we'll ... then you'll sleep over
          and then in the morning ...
                    (driving herself into a complex)
          ... you'll be distant and you won't be
          ... able to stay for breakfast ...
          you'll just have some coffee maybe ...

                    PARRY
          I don't drink coffee.

                    LYDIA
          And then we'll exchange phone numbers
          and you'll leave and never call and I'll
          go to work and feel great for the first
          hour and then slowly turn into a piece
          of dirt by lunch. Why am I putting
          myself through this?
                    (to PARRY, as she quickens her
                    pace)
          It was very nice ... uh, meeting you.
          Good night ...

She walks quickly away. PARRY stops, confused to say the
least, then runs after her. LYDIA is just about to enter the
front door of her building when PARRY stops her.

                                        (CONTINUED)

                              PARRY
                    Excuse me ...

                              LYDIA
                    Listen, I'm not feeling well.

                              PARRY
                    Well, no wonder. We just met, made love
                    and broke up all in the space of thirty
                    seconds and I can't even remember the
                    first kiss which is the best part.

                              LYDIA
                    Listen, you're very nice ... b ...

                              PARRY
                    So are you, but I think maybe you should
                    shut up now ...
                              (LYDIA is surprised)
                    ... I'm not coming up to your apartment.
                    That was never my idea.

                              LYDIA
                    Oh ... You mean you don't want to.

                              PARRY
                              (deeply sincere)
                    Oh no, I want to.
                              (sweetly)
                    I've got a hard-on for you the size of
                    Florida ... but I don't ... want just
                    one night. I have a confession to make.

                              LYDIA
                    You're married.

                              PARRY
                    No.

                              LYDIA
                    Divorced.

                              PARRY
                    No, I ...

                              LYDIA
                    You have a disease.

                              PARRY
                    Will you stop! ...
                              (pause, he looks at her)
                    ... I'm in love with you ...

LYDIA is about to speak when PARRY puts his hand over her
mouth.

                                                    (CONTINUED)

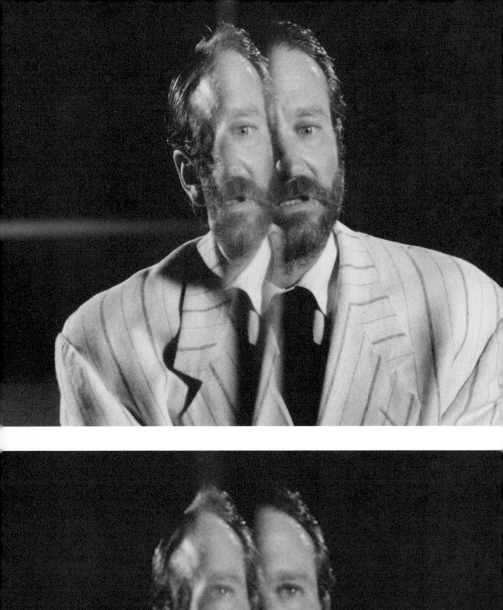

                              PARRY
                         (continuing)
          ... It's not just from tonight. I've
          known you for a long time. I see you
          come out of work every day. I walk with
          you to lunch. I know what you order ...
          I see you buy Baby Ruths before going
          back in ...
                         (slowly removes his hand)
          I know how you feel on certain days by
          whether or not you go into the
          bookstore ...
                         (LYDIA listens with fascination)
          ... I know you hate your job and you
          don't have many friends and you some-
          times feel like you're not as ... as
          wonderful as everybody else and you're a
          little uncoordinated ...
                         (LYDIA begins to cry)
          ... and feeling like you're the only one
          who's as separate and ... alone as you
          are ... and I love you. I love you. I
          think you're the greatest thing since
          ... spice racks and I would be knocked
          out several times if I even got just a
          first kiss. But I'll be back in the
          morning. And I won't be distant. And I
          will call if you let me ... But I still
          don't drink coffee.

                              LYDIA
          Shhh ...

She kisses him, tentatively — almost awkwardly. PARRY feels
a surge of emotion that make his whole body tremble. LYDIA
separates from him an looks into his eyes. She pinches his
cheek, hard.

                              LYDIA
                         (continuing, earnestly)
          You *are* real, aren't you?

They kiss again. Then LYDIA quickly pulls away.

                              LYDIA
                         (continuing)
          ... You can call ...

She runs into the building, afraid to linger and ruin the
moment. PARRY stands transfixed, his eyes following her.

LYDIA pauses briefly to look back. She is so excited. She
smiles and turns toward the elevator ... her skirt spinning
with her.

CUT TO;

74   INT.   LYDIA'S BUILDING — SECONDS LATER

She re-enacts the entire love scene in her mind, to make
sure it went as well as she thinks.

CUT TO:

75   EXT.   LYDIA'S BUILDING — NIGHT

PARRY is standing frozen. We don't know whether he's looking
ahead of him or in his mind's eye. He appears anxious and
frightened as he steps back, away from LYDIA's building. He
senses someone is watching him. PARRY smiles. But suddenly
it is as if everything has gone into slow motion. His eyes
focus on her skirt as it swirls as she turns. His expression
grows dark: O.S. we hear a horse's hooves moving in slowly
as CAMERA moves to closeup. He slowly turns his head and
looks down the block to the corner to see the RED KNIGHT. He
sits upon his horse as if waiting for PARRY. The street
lamps cast a glow around his imposing figure. The night air
lifts his cape up around his massive shoulders.

PARRY, vulnerable, afraid, whispers plainly:

> PARRY
> Let me have this.

CUT TO:

THE RED KNIGHT, silent, unforgiving, unrelenting.

PARRY begins to move away, taking a step back and then
another and another until he is running down toward the
other corner.

The RED KNIGHT shifts his horse to PARRY's direction and
begins to charge. PARRY runs through the deserted city
streets — running for his life; the sounds of the RED KNIGHT
galloping grows closer. The RED KNIGHT looks like a surreal
figure hunting his prey.

As PARRY runs, IMAGES/MEMORIES begin to flood his mind
uncontrollably.

75A   EXT.   HOSPITAL — NIGHT

An ambulance arriving at a hospital — his wounded WIFE being
moved on a stretcher.

CUT BACK TO:

75B   EXT.   LYDIA'S STREET — NIGHT

PARRY running away from the KNIGHT.

75C INT. **BABBITT'S — NIGHT**

PARRY and his WIFE at the side bar. He is making her laugh uncontrollably. He sees EDWIN in the doorway, making nothing of it.

CUT TO:

75D EXT. **STREET — NIGHT**

PARRY still running.

> PARRY
> *Sstttoppp!!!*

PASSERS-BY on the street witness the familiar sight of a bum screaming at thin air and then turn away. We hear the galloping getting louder.

PARRY runs, mumbling incoherently. PEOPLE on the street get out of his way or snicker behind his back. The RED KNIGHT gallops toward PARRY as he runs, his face wet with tears — yet contorting with angry, incomprehensible reprisals. PEOPLE on the street pay no attention.

CUT TO:

75E EXT. **BABBITT'S — NIGHT**

A bar with broken glass surrounded by POLICE and SPECTATORS.

75F EXT. **CENTRAL PARK — DAY**

PARRY and his WIFE waltzing. Closeup on their clasped hands as PARRY maneuvers a ring onto her finger.

75G INT. **BABBITT'S — NIGHT**

His WIFE's lifeless hand lifted onto the stretcher.

76 EXT. **CENTRAL PARK — DAY**

Surprised, PARRY's WIFE stops dancing to look at the ring. PARRY smiles. It is his proposal.

77 EXT. **BABBITT'S — NIGHT**

Ambulance driving away with PARRY holding his WIFE's hand in the back.

78   EXT.   CENTRAL PARK — DAY

Dancing, his WIFE embraces him as she accepts.

79   INT.   TV NEWS STATION — NIGHT

JACK's face on a TV news broadcast with a reporter
commenting.

                                                    CUT TO:

80   EXT.   EAST RIVER PROMENADE — NIGHT

PARRY has run all the way to the promenade along the river.

                        PARRY
            *Come on! ... Where are you!!! Where are
            you!!*
                    (softer, dropping to his knees)
            Where are you ...

81   EXT.   THE END OF THE PROMENADE — NIGHT

The two juvenile delinquents, LEATHER and WINDBREAKER, come
strutting down the promenade in slow motion. PARRY looks
toward them, as if surrendering.

Through PARRY's POV we see the two YOUTHS are being led by
the RED KNIGHT on his horse.

PARRY, tear-stained face, rises to meet them. The YOUTHS
reach PARRY and surround him. LEATHER flicks open a
switchblade.

                        LEATHER
            ... We're tired of looking at you
            people ...

PARRY stands before them, surrendering to his fate.

Throught his POV, the RED KNIGHT is pointing a sword at him
in front of LEATHER and his switchblade. He slashes at
PARRY's chest as we:

                                                    CUT TO:

WIDE ANGLE OF THE PROMENADE, as PARRY sinks to his knees.
The YOUTHS close in around him.

                                                    CUT TO:

82   INT.   ANNE'S APARTMENT — MORNING

Outside the bathroom door, we hear the toilet flush. ANNE

                                            (CONTINUED)

100

exits in an imitation silk kimono, feeling very much the
satisfied woman. She crosses into the living room and finds
JACK, on the phone in mid-conversation, beside his open box
of radio tapes. She hugs him from behing as he talks, still
warm from their all-night lovemaking.

> JACK
> (excited, very "on")
> ... Well, ya know, I'm feeling good, Lou
> ... I don't know how else to put it ...
> I ... I had some personal things to work
> out and ... And I have and ...
> (listens, then:)
> Yeah ... well, the thing is ... I want
> to work again ... I want to get back
> into it ... You think that's possible?

ANNE releases her hug, looking surprised, pleased, impressed
— she stands by, waiting to ask JACK what's up.

> JACK
> (to phone)
> I understand ...
> (obedient)
> I am ... I won't ... I will ...
> (beaming)
> *Great!* Thanks a lot, Lou ... Tuesday's
> fine.
> (listens)
> Okay ... thanks ...

He hangs up the phone elated. ANNE can't wait to hear.

> ANNE
> So what's going on? Who's Lou again?

> JACK
> (disappointed she doesn't
> remember)
> My agent. I called my agent.

> ANNE
> You're kidding! What did he say?

> JACK
> He says if I want to get back to work,
> no problem. He wants me to come in and
> talk and ... and ... *that's it!*

> ANNE
> *Whoah!* Oh, honey, that's terrific!

She gives him a big hug. JACK is the first to break away.

> JACK
> (organizing his tapes)
> I've got to put these tapes in some kind
> (MORE)

(CONTINUED)

101

>   JACK (CONTINUED)
>   of order ... and ... Oh, I should get my
>   sport jacket cleaned ...
>   (he crosses to the closet)
>   ... There's coffee if you want ...

>   ANNE
>   *You* made coffee? ... You're going back
>   to work *and* you made coffee? ... I love
>   this!

JACK does not respond as he looks through the closet. ANNE
gets her coffee and sits watching JACK move about so full of
energy and focus.

>   ANNE
>   (continuing)
>   It's so great to see you like this,
>   honey ... I can't tell you!

>   JACK
>   (looking at jacket)
>   Thanks.

>   ANNE
>   (she smiles and drinks)
>   Ya know, I'm thinkin' — with another
>   income coming in, I would love to get a
>   bigger place.

JACK stops organizing for a beat.

>   ANNE
>   (continuing)
>   ... I don't want to rush things — you
>   have to get a job first, but I'm so sure
>   that's gonna happen I'm not even
>   thinking about it.

JACK brings out his sports jacket, then returns to his
tapes, hoping he can avoid having to respond.

>   JACK
>   Ugh, these tapes are a mess. I don't
>   know where to begin ...

>   ANNE
>   ... I would love to start looking at
>   least. You know, maybe a two bedroom or
>   even, maybe the top floor of a house —
>   like in Brooklyn or Staten Island ...

JACK looks at her, not knowing what to say.

>   ANNE
>   (continuing)
>   ... What? ... You don't want to commute?

                                              (CONTINUED)

>   JACK
>   No, it's not ... Come here ...

He turns her around and cuddles her up in his arms, with her
back to him.

>   JACK
>   (continuing)
>   You're an incredible woman, Anne ...

ANNE beaks away suddenly and looks at him, sternly.

>   JACK
>   (continuing)
>   What?

>   ANNE
>   "I'm an incredible woman?" What is this,
>   a death sentence?

>   JACK
>   No, I ... I think we should talk about
>   this.

>   ANNE
>   (aware and suspicious)
>   You want to talk? Come on, Jack ... Did
>   I cross the line by mentioning the
>   future or what?

>   JACK
>   No ... it's just ...

ANNE shifts her body to face him directly.

>   JACK
>   (continuing)
>   ... Listen, so much has happened and I
>   think it would be a good thing for both
>   of us if we slowed things down a little.

>   ANNE
>   Slowed things down? Where have I been?
>   Have we been going fast!?

>   JACK
>   Right now, I'm just not sure about ...
>   making such definite plans.

Pause. ANNE stares at him like he's speaking Dutch.

>   ANNE
>   I'm lost. What are you saying?

JACK sits them both down, takes her hand in his, takes a
breath.

(CONTINUED)

> JACK
> It's been a real ... real difficult time
> for me ... the past year or so ... And
> now, for the first time, Anne, I feel
> like I'm above water. I feel like I know
> a lot more than I did, and I don't want
> to make any mistakes so ... I think what
> I need is some time ... to make the
> right choices. And ... I think that
> maybe ... I need to be alone for a
> while.

ANNE is speechless — for the moment.

> JACK
> ... I'd like to focus on my career — now
> that I can, now that everything's all
> right ... Parry's taken care of ... and
> ... Like I said, I feel like I know a
> lot more now and I don't ...

> ANNE
> (interrupts; getting upset)
> First of all, let me tell you something
> — you don't know shit. Second of all, as
> far as *we* go, what time do you need?
> What have we been doing here, except
> *time*? Have I ever ... ever pressured
> you!?

> JACK
> No.

> ANNE
> No. So what time do you need? I love you
> — you love me — you want to get your
> career going, great! I'd like to be a
> part of it — I think I deserve that! So
> what do you need time to figure out
> alone!?

JACK doesn't answer. Pause. ANNE is afraid she knows.

> ANNE
> (continuing)
> All right. I'm going to ask you one
> question.
> (summoning up all her strength)
> Do you love me?

Pause.

> JACK
> I don't know.

(CONTINUED)

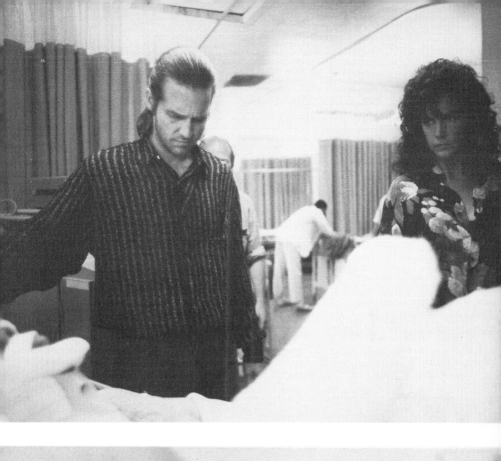

She slaps him.

> ANNE
> You can't even give me that?! What were
> you gonna do, Jack ... just organize
> your life ...
>   (indicates the box)
> ... walk out that door, move in by
> yourself then what — drop the news when
> you find somebody else? What were you
> planning to do, Jack?

> JACK
> I didn't know. I just said all I want is
> some time.

> ANNE
>   (fighting back the tears)
> Bullshit! If you're going to hurt me,
> you hurt me now — not some long ...
> drawn out hurt that takes weeks of my
> life because you don't have the balls!

> JACK
>   (pause, then:)
> All right ... I'll pack my stuff
> tonight.

ANNE slaps him again.

> ANNE
> What have you been doing here! *Huh! I
> wanna know! What have you been doing
> here?!*

> JACK
> *Listen!* We both got something out of it,
> all right!

> ANNE
> Oh yeah? What did I get? What did I get
> I couldn't've gotten from somebody with
> no name any night of the week? You think
> your company is such a treat? Your
> moods, your ...
>   (sarcastic)
> "pain," your problems ... You think
> you're entertaining?

> JACK
> Then what do you want to stay with me
> for?

ANNE physically attacks him.

                                        (CONTINUED)

> ANNE
> BECAUSE I LOVE YOU! ... STUPID! ...
> FUCKIN'! ...

JACK blocks her blows and holds her arms. ANNE surrenders to her tears. He is about to embrace her, when she pulls away.

> ANNE
> No ... you don't get to be nice now. I'm not gonna play some game with you where we act like friends so you can walk out of here feeling good about yourself. I'm not a liar. If you're gonna leave me then that's what we call it.

The phone rings. JACK answers it.

> JACK
> Hello? ... Yeah ... My wallet? What do you mean? ...
> (his face drops)
> What? ... What? ...

84   INT.   **HOSPITAL WARD — NIGHT**

PARRY lies in bed — his face bandaged, his arms in casts, his chest tightly wrapped. He has been severely beaten. JACK and ANNE stand at the foot of the bed in shock. A DOCTOR appears. The DOCTOR is young, dedicated and inexperienced enough to still feel compassion.

> JACK
> Parry?

> DOCTOR
> He can't hear you.
> (JACK and ANNE turn)
> Hi ... I'm Dr. Weintraub ...
> (shakes hands)
> I was on duty when they brought him in ... I've been going over his record ... He was brought in once before, I understand ...
> (reads)
> ... "catatonic stupor" ... condition rendered him non-verbal for a period of ...

> JACK
> Yeah, so? The guy's beat up — he — he probably has a concussion or something, right?
> (DOCTOR doesn't reply)
> He'll snap out of it?

(CONTINUED)

                    DOCTOR
I'm afraid not ... then again, I'm not
sure. The beating's bad but it's not the
problem ... It seems he's ... re-
experiencing the catatonia ... So, like
before, he could snap out of it in an
hour or in thirteen months or thirteen
years ... I don't know. There's no way
to tell.

                    JACK
But ... how could that happen?

                    DOCTOR
Well, it's not usual in his case ...
Sometimes victims of tragedies are
subject to the brain's replay system.
The brain never loses anything — it just
stores it up and waits. A person could
actually re-experience the full effect
of a tragedy long after the event took
place. I was reading how he lost his
wife ... Are you relatives?
          (JACK shakes his head)
Well, it doesn't matter. We'll take care
of it. He'll have to be sent back to the
same institution ...
          (he checks the record)

                    JACK
What if I was a relative?

                    DOCTOR
You'd have the option to care for him at
home but my advice is it wouldn't be the
best thing for him. He needs hospital
care. I just thought you could sign the
release forms, but the city can do that.
I wouldn't feel responsible in any way.
There's really nothing you can do. I'm
sorry.

With that, the DOCTOR exits. JACK and ANNE face PARRY.

                    ANNE
Just like a guy. Finds the woman of his
dreams then falls into a coma ... Poor
Lydia ...
          (she looks at JACK)
... Some women just have no luck, huh?

Including herself in this remark, and having cried all she
could cry, she and JACK exchange one final look. ANNE turns
and, with all her dignity, walks out of the ward. After a
beat:

                                        (CONTINUED)

107

>   JACK
>   Anne ... Anne ... I'll call you, O.K.?

But ANNE doesn't stop or turn — she keeps walking. JACK
stares at PARRY. CAMERA moves into C.U. — his face hardening
into a mixture of hurt, rage and resignation.

SUPER — SIX MONTHS LATER

86   INT.   RADIO STUDIO — DAY

CAMERA pans the studio as JACK signs off his broadcast.

>   JACK
>   Well, I'm gone ... Have a perfect
>   weekend and remember on Monday, we have
>   as our studio guest, Ben Starr — star of
>   the recently defunct hit TV show "On The
>   Radio." It's the rise and fall story of
>   one of television's brightest stars
>   ruined by charges of sodomy in an
>   Atlanta airport men's room. If you often
>   wonder, "What IS sodomy exactly?" Ben'll
>   have that answer and many more for you
>   on Monday's show. ... Until then, don't
>   do anything that will break your pattern
>   of being the selfish scum sucking race
>   you are. From one of the Botched to all
>   of you bungled cats out there, I love ya
>   and right back at cha! Over and out!

He flicks his monitor off as a commercial takes over. The
CREW works in silence behind him. He rubs his tired face and
sits there.

CAMERA PAUSES on JACK for a moment as he sits in silence. He
looks neither happy nor sad, neither satisfied nor unsatis-
fied. He looks blank — emotionless — as if he knows something is lacking but he hasn't the strength or interest to
find out. The phone rings, breaking the silence. JACK picks
it up.

>   JACK
>   Yeah ... Yeah Lou ...
>   (no excitement, no energy
>   until:)
>   Lou, I said I want an offer or they can
>   forget it ... Well, tell them I'm
>   meeting with the cable people about a
>   talk show and ... What? ... Beth's
>   father set it up ... No, he owns it.
>   Fuck you, Lou ... And if the network is
>   (MORE)

                                                  (CONTINUED)

>   JACK (CONTINUED)
>   ready to make me an offer and I see a
>   script, then fine ... otherwise, forget
>   it ...

He hangs up.

>   BETH (O.C.)
>   Hi ...

JACK turns to see his new improved girlfriend, BETH — a
tall, statuesque redhead in a smart Chanel outfit. BETH
crosses to him and they kiss. When they kiss, all the lights
in the surrounding studio booths go out, as the CREW heads
home. JACK's studio is now surrounded by blackness. After
the kiss, JACK gets right to business.

>   JACK
>   Hi ... Did you talk to your father?

>   BETH
>   (hiding good news)
>   Yeeesss ...

>   JACK
>   (slightly annoyed by her
>   coquettish game)
>   Weeelll!

>   BETH
>   Well, Daddy said ... and this is word
>   for word ... He said ... that he thought
>   ... that you were a home run.

JACK knows this must mean a great deal — especially to BETH
— but he just can't get steam up. He smiles weakly.

>   JACK
>   Great.

>   BETH
>   Really. He thinks you'll be a phenomenal
>   success ... and he says the cable people
>   are very excited about the meeting ... I
>   said I always knew that and I really
>   think it was like the first time he
>   really respected me ... So thank you for
>   that.

JACK nods "it was nothing" as his hands move up her body.

>   BETH
>   (continuing)
>   Oh and I called him later to thank him
>   but I really think you should send him a
>   (MORE)

>   (CONTINUED)

> BETH (CONTINUED)
> note ... He wants to take us out to
> dinner tonight. The car's picking us up
> at seven ...

JACK nods and watches BETH's breasts pressing against her
dress. Turned on, JACK moves to her and begins fondling her,
as he kisses her neck. BETH giggles.

> BETH
> Jaaack ... what are you, crazy? There're
> people all around us.

JACK flips a switch that sends his studio into darkness and
continues kissing and fondling. BETH giggles some more.

> BETH
> Jaaack ... I can't do this ...

JACK begins to ease her to the floor. BETH stops him.

> BETH
> What is this thing you have with the
> floor?

They lower O.C. We hear BETH continue O.C.

> BETH (O.C.)
> Oh it's cold ... I'm cold ... honey ...
> Jack, can we please do this after dinner
> ... in bed ... like normal people? ... I
> really want you but I'll want you more
> later, O.K. I promise.

CUT TO:

87A   EXT.   MIDTOWN OFFICE BUILDING — DAY

A STREET BUM, whose face we cannot see, is busy asking
people for change, but no one is stopping. A SECURITY GUARD
exits the building and starts yelling at the BUM to leave. A
cab pulls up and out step JACK and LOU. They start walking
toward the building when the BUM recognizes JACK.

> BUM
> JACK! ... JACK! ...

JACK turns as the BUM starts for him. Simultaneously, the
SECURITY GUARD intercepts the BUM, who JACK recognizes as
the GAY BUM from Central Park.

> GAY BUM
> JACK! ... JACK! IT'S MEE ... REMEMBER ME
> ... YOU KNOW ME!

> GUARD
> GET OUTTA HERE I SAID!! ...

(CONTINUED)

LOU tries to usher JACK into the building, but JACK stands
frozen for a moment, as the GUARD pulls out a club and
starts poking the GAY BUM away. JACK doesn't know what to
do.

> LOU
> You KNOW that guy!?

JACK doesn't answer.

> GAY BUM
> JACK ... JACK ... PLEASE, CAN I TALK TO
> YOU? I JUST NEED ... I NEED TO TALK TO
> YOU, JACK ... I ...

But the GUARD keeps at him. JACK realizes people are
watching him and he enters the building with LOU as the GAY
BUM screams:

> GAY BUM
> JACK ... PLEASE ... JAAAAAACCKKK!!!!
> JAACCK! ... WHY WON'T ANYBODY ... WHAT'S
> THE MATTER ...

But JACK disappears inside . The GAY BUM is blocked by the
GUARD. He throws his arms up and starts muttering to himself
helplessly.

                                                    CUT TO:

87B   INT.   OFFICE BUILDING — NETWORK OFFICES — DAY

A hyperkinetic TV EXEC is pitching JACK, who sits next to
LOU.

> TV EXEC
> It's a weekly comedy about the homeless.

JACK can't believe his fate. He looks to a coffee table and
sees a magazine front page: LANGDON CARMICHAEL BUYS VAN
GOGH'S ROAD WITH CYPRESSES FOR 20 MILLION DOLLARS. CAMERA
PANS TO C.U.

> TV EXEC
>   (continuing)
> ... But it's not depressing in any way.
> We want to find a funny. upbeat way of
> bringing up the issue of homeless to
> television. There are three wacky
> homeless characters but they're wise ...
> they're wacky and they're wise ... And
> the hook is, they love being homeless.
> They love the freedom ... they love the
> adventure ... It's all about the joy of
> living ... not all the bullshit we have
> to deal with ... the money, the politics
> ... the pressures ... And we're gonna
> call it "Home Free" ...

                                          (CONTINUED)

111

87B   CONTINUED:

> LOU
> Oooooo ... I got a rush ...

Suddenly, JACK stands up and bolts out of the room.

> TV EXEC
> What? ... Where is he ... Lou , is this
> another disappearing act with this guy
> or what?

> LOU
> (overlapping)
> I'm sure it's nothing ... He probably
> had to go to the bathroom ... I'll find
> out ...

CUT TO:

87C   **EXT.   OFFICE BUILDING (101 PARK AVE. SO) — DAY**

JACK rushes out of the building to find the GAY BUM, but
he's gone.

CUT TO:

89   **INT.   PARRY's BASEMENT — DAY**

JACK walks around, He looks at the wall of weapons and the
mural of the medieval scene. He looks through the maps,
ropes, plans for the robbery. He finds the Pinnochio doll
still keeping guard before the Red Knight wall of
scribblings.

89A   **EXT.   A LOT BENEATH THE MANHATTAN BRIDGE — DARK**

JACK approaches the entrance to the lot from the street,
carrying an open box of assorted deli food and coffee. He
stops in the entrance and looks at the deserted lot.

Gone are the little cliques of homeless, once scattered
throughout the place. Gone is the magic and danger that
night cast upon the surroundings. All JACK sees is garbage
and decay.

Suddenly, SIRENS from an ambulance pull his attention away.
At the same time, the BLACK and the IRISHMAN (from that same
first night with PARRY) come running out from between the
two giant foundations of the bridge and bolt out of the lot.
JACK smiles in recognition as he moves to block them.

> JACK
> Hey! Hey, guys! ... Remember me ...

But the BLACK and the IRISHMAN push him out of the way ...

(CONTINUED)

112

> BLACK
> Let me the fuck alone, goddamn it ...

> IRISHMAN
> (overlapping)
> Move it, for Christ sakes. *Move* ... *!!!*

The IRISHMAN shoves JACK against the fence and runs, with the BLACK close behind. They disappear underneath the highway as JACK turns and sees an ambulance pulling up to the sight. PARAMEDICS wheel a gurney from the ambulance, past JACK and into the lot between the giant foundations. JACK approaches with great trepidation. He moves into view just in time to see the PARAMEDICS lift the body of the HIPPY BUM onto the stretcher.

> JACK
> Hey ... *Hey* ... Hey wait, I know him ...

The PARAMEDICS stop. JACK approaches the gurney. The HIPPY's eyes are open and glazed.

> JACK
> (continuing)
> Hey ... hey, remember me ... Marvel
> Comics, right? ... Remember Parry ... Su-
> perbum? Remember you guys saved my ass ...

> PARAMEDIC
> Mister, he's dead.

JACK realizes the glazed eyes are actually dead eyes. The PARAMEDICS wheel him away.

> CUT TO:

90   INT.   **OAKBROOK INSTITUTE — THAT NIGHT**

JACK approaches the nurses' station when he spots a familiar face — LYDIA.

We can see a change in her; the self-consciousness replaced with a self-assurance, the insecurity replaced with maturity. She wears a handsome tailored suit. JACK hides from her and listens.

> LYDIA
> (to NURSE)
> Excuse me, but I brought new bed sheets
> for him last week. They were lime colored
> with little watermelons on them ...

> NURSE
> Oh yes ... I'm sorry. They're being
> cleaned. The doctor had a little
> accident with a hypo.

> (CONTINUED)

>   LYDIA
>   All right ... Make sure he gets them,
>   okay? thank you.

JACK watches her exit.

91   **INT.   PARRY'S WARD — NIGHT**

JACK enters a room lined up on both sides with beds and
PATIENTS.

The various PATIENTS — all men — are confined to their beds.
Some are mumbling inaudibly to themselves, others are
rocking back and forth, others just stare off into space.
PARRY sits in a bed — his eyes are dead, his body unrespon-
sive. JACK sits at the foot of his bed. PARRY does not
respond.

>   JACK
>   *Hi!* ... It's Jack ... How are you doing?
>   ... you look good ... You do.

PARRY remains the same. Other PATIENTS look at JACK as if
he's nuts talking to a catatonic person. JACK moves closer
to him. He picks up his hand and holds it. Then shakes it.

>   JACK
>   (continuing)
>   ... Hey ... You gonna wake up for me?
>   Huh? ...

No response. JACK leans closer to him. His tone changes.

>   JACK
>   (continuing)
>   ... This isn't over, is it? ... You
>   think you're going to make me do this,
>   don't you? ...
>   (sternly)
>   Well, forget it! No fucking way! ... I
>   don't feel responsible for you, or for
>   any of them! Everybody has bad things
>   happen to them ... I'm not God. I don't
>   decide ... People survive.
>   (beat)
>   Say something!?

The other PATIENTS stop their mumblings and watch, as if
JACK were an interesting TV show. JACK paces before the bed.

>   JACK
>   (continuing)
>   ... Everything's been going great!
>   *Great!* I'm ... I'm gonna have my own
>   (MORE)

                                              (CONTINUED)

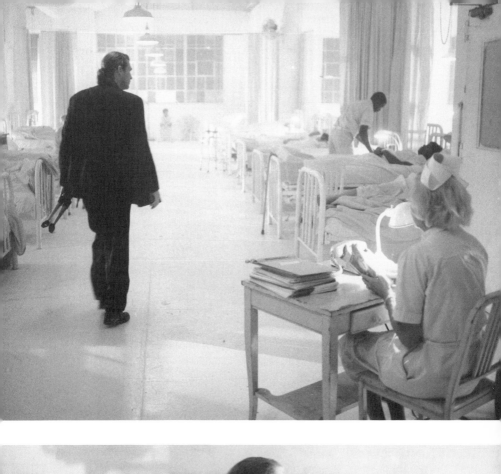

                        JACK (CONTINUED)
          cable talk show, with an incredible
          equity I might add ... I ... I ... have
          an ... an incredibly gorgeous fucking
          girlfriend ... I ... I am living an
          incredible fucking life!!! ... So don't
          lay there in your comfortable little
          coma and think I'm about to risk all of
          that because I feel responsible for you!
                    (to the other PATIENTS)
          I am not responsible!
                    (to PARRY)
          And I don't feel guilty ... You've got
          it easy.
                    (intensely)
          I'm out there every day. Every day
          trying to figure out what the hell I'm
          doing ... why, no matter what I have, it
          feels like I have nothing ... So don't
          think I feel sorry for you! It's easy
          being nuts! Try being me! ...
                    (beat)
          So I won't do this. I do not believe in
          this. And don't give me that stuff about
          *being the one! There is nothing ...
          nothing special about me!* I control my
          own destiny — not some overweight
          fairies. I say what I'm going to do and
          *I am not risking my life to get some
          fucking cup for some fucking vegetable*
          ... And even if I did do this, I want
          you to know it wouldn't be because I had
          to! It wouldn't be 'cause I feel guilty
          or cursed or ... or ... bad or
          responsible or anything ...

The tears come. JACK gently pushes the hair off PARRY's
face.

                        JACK
                    (continuing)
          Aw shit ... If I do this ... and I mean
          IF! ... It's because I want to do this
          ... for you. That's all!! For you!
                    (he kisses PARRY's forehead)
          Don't go anywhere ... huh?

                                                    CUT TO:

92   **EXT.   CARMICHAEL TOWNHOUSE — MIDDLE OF THE NIGHT**

JACK stands on the deserted block. He looks around at the
neighboring houses — all the New Yorkers safely locked away
behind their doors, intentionally oblivious to what goes on
around them. JACK is holding a rope with a self-made hook.

                                              (CONTINUED)

He looks up at the building, takes a gulp, then throws the rope up. It misses and falls back toward him — scaring him to the side and making an awful sound when it lands. JACK tries again. It catches. He tugs a bit. He begins to climb up the building.

> JACK
> Thank god I live in a city where nobody looks up ...

He places a foot on the wall and begins to climb, mumbling:

> JACK
> What the hell am I doing? Can't fuckin'
> believe this is my life!
>   (imitates a whiny PARRY)
> "Oh, Jack, you're the one ... we have to
> get the Grail." I'll give ya Grail, ya
> stupid dingbat! Climbing up walls in the
> middle of the goddamn city — in the
> middle of the goddamn night while that
> schmuck lays in bed dreaming about
> Camelot! I live through this and I'll be
> the King of the Idiots ... What a
> fucking honor!

He pulls and steps, pulls and steps — climbing up to a balcony midway between the street and the roof. JACK climbs over, falling into some exterior lighting that lines the balcony.

A light is jarred loose, falling to the ground making an awful SOUND and lighting a stained glass window. JACK raises his eyes and sees the RED KNIGHT standing six feet tall, as pictured in the design of the stained glass window. He stares until he hears the SOUND OF A HORSE GALLOPING. He freezes, then cautiously looks toward the street — but the street is vacant. The galloping stops. An eerie silence hangs in the air.

> JACK
> Oh great. This is great. I'm hearing
> horses now. Parry will be so pleased.
>   (he picks up the rope and throws
>   it to the roof)
> RADIO PERSONALITY TURNS SCREWBALL ON
> MISSION FROM GOD ... I just hope when
> they put me away they find me a bed
> right next to his!

He begins to climb from the balcony to the roof. Suddenly JACK hears a siren in the distance and freezes, closing his eyes.

92PT SUDDENLY, THREE POLICE CARS come barreling down the street —

(CONTINUED)

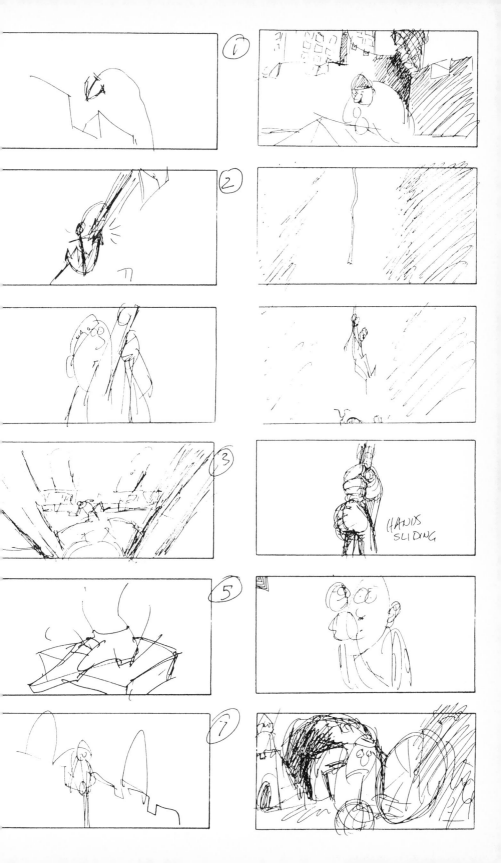

sirens blasting, they screech to a halt. A dozen cops hit
the streets with rifles and spotlights aimed at JACK. A
REPORTER faces a news camera (the same REPORTER from EDWIN's
T.V. news report).

> REPORTER
> A crazed radio personality dangles from
> the townhouse of a billionaire ...

ANNE jumps out of a police car and runs to the townhouse —
her face full of love and concern.

> ANNE
> Jack!

JACK opens his eyes.

93   POV

The street is empty. The siren was from an ambulance that
drives off in the distance. There are no cops, no spotlights
and no Anne.

> JACK
> (quietly)
> Anne.

                                               CUT TO:

94   EXT.   CARMICHAEL TOWNHOUSE — ROOF — NIGHT

JACK reaches the roof and climbs over. He pulls the rope up
and quickly moves to the skylight. He looks down into it and
sees a dark void. He takes a breath and pulls out some
masking tape. He makes three big tape loops and applies them
to the glass. He then takes out a glass cutter and begins to
cut a pane. The sound, at first, is startling. An O.S. VOICE
says:

> VOICE (O.S.)
> You're being too loud.

JACK's heart stops. He looks into the darkness of the roof
but sees nothing. He tries to slow down his heart and shake
away thoughts of demons in the dark. He continues cutting.
When he finishes the entire pane, he replaces the cutter in
his pocket then plasters his arm against the tape. He gently
bangs the pane and it comes loose, sticking to tape. He
is impressed. He places the pane on the roof and, fastening
one end of the rope to a pipe, lowers the other end down.

                                               CUT TO:

95   INT.   CARMICHAEL TOWNHOUSE — NIGHT

JACK eases himself down into a pitch black room, but the
rope doesn't reach the floor. He dangles for a moment,
fearful of falling until he realizes it is the only way to

                                               (CONTINUED)

get down. He takes a breath and releases, falling to the
floor with a thud. The room is dark. The moonlight barely
illuminates the austere, castle-like surroundings. JACK
pulls out the page from the *Architecture Today* and lights a
lighter. The "Grail" is in the library on the first floor.
JACK cautiously makes his way out.

96   INT.   FIFTH FLOOR OF THE TOWNHOUSE — NIGHT

JACK looks down the dark hallway. At the far end he can see
the top of a staircase. He heads toward it until he sees
something that makes him stop dead in his tracks.

Slowly, a SHADOW holding a shotgun emerges up the stairs
against the back wall. JACK is paralyzed. He closes his
eyes. The SHADOW reaches the top of the landing. It is EDWIN
MALNICK — waering the same expression we saw on the TV
broadcast — sad and harmless. JACK's heart is bursting out
of his chest. EDWIN calmly raises the gun, cocks it and
fires. The shot blasts down the hallway, deafening JACK. But
when he opens his eyes to see if he has been hit, There is
no blood, no wound — and when he looks up, no EDWIN. He
pulls himself together and continues.

CUT TO:

97   INT.   FIRST FLOOR OF TOWNHOUSE — NIGHT

JACK enters CARMICHAEL's library carefully. A small lamp is
lit on a small table beside a large Chesterfield chair,
which is turned facing the fireplace. JACK spots the antique
commode and crosses to it. Within the commode, sitting
innocently behind two small glass doors, is the "Grail."
JACK gently opens the doors and takes out the goblet. He
holds it reverently for a moment, then, noticing an
inscription, reads:

TO LITTLE LANNIE CARMICHAEL FOR ALL HIS HARD WORK ... P.S.
247 CHRISTMAS PAGEANT 1932.

JACK can't help but smile. He takes the chalice and turns,
when suddenly he notices the bare foot of a man sticking out
from in front of the Chesterfield chair. JACK slowly moves
around the large back of the chair to the front and sees, to
his amazement, LANGDON CARMICHAEL, wearing only his silk
pajama bottoms, asleep on the chair. On the table beside him
is an empty bottle of vodka and an empty bottle of pills.

JACK doesn't know what to do, when it suddenly strikes him
that CARMICHAEL hasn't moved at all. At first he thinks it's
another hallucination, but then he notices the pill bottle.
He takes a step toward it, the floor squeaking beneath him,

(CONTINUED)

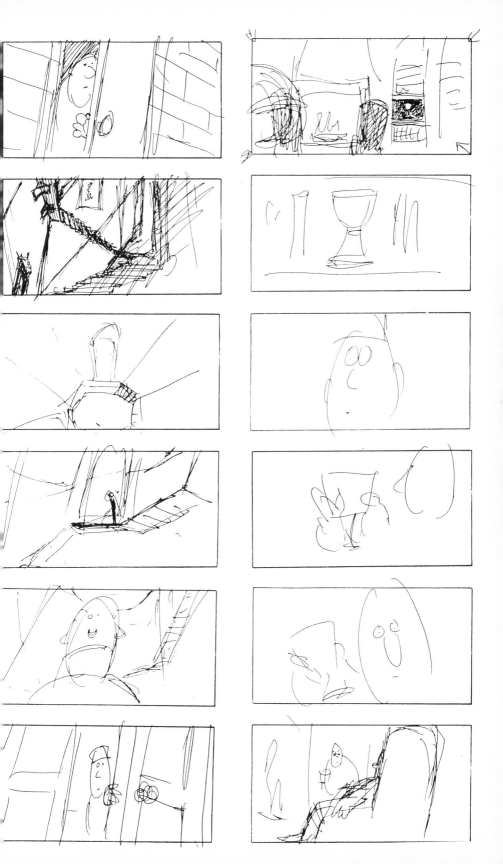

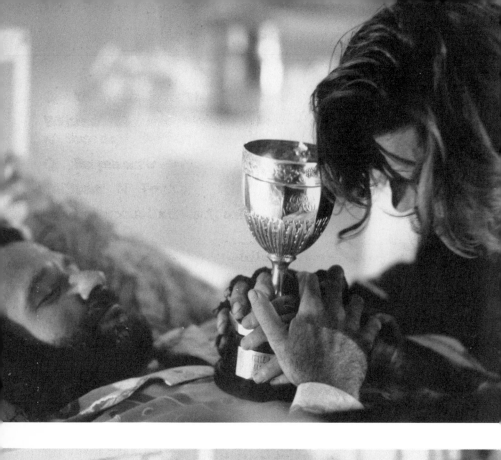
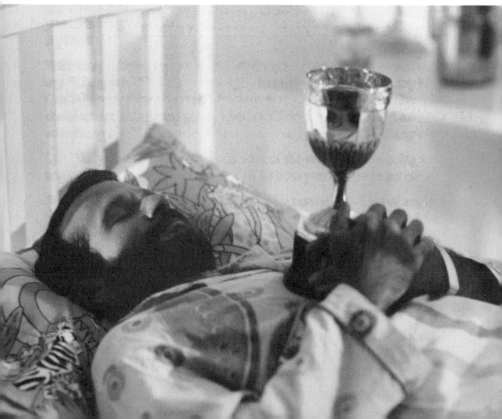

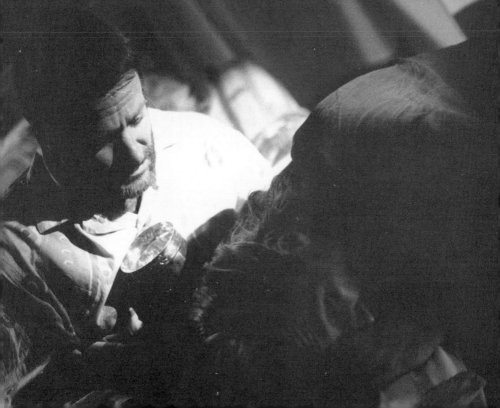

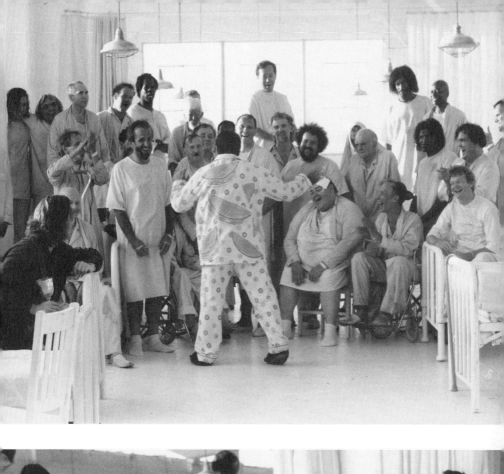

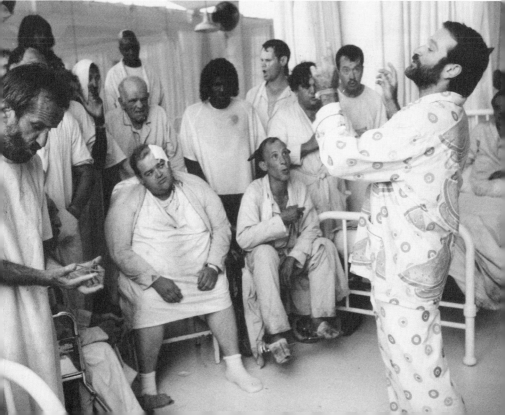

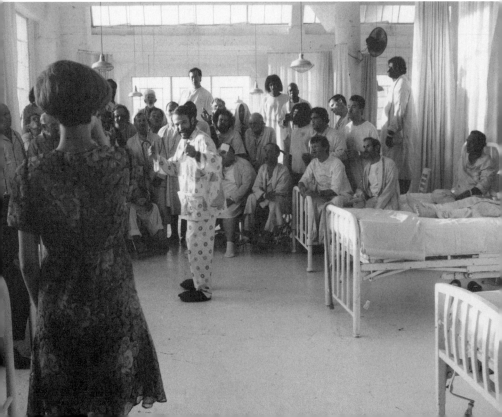

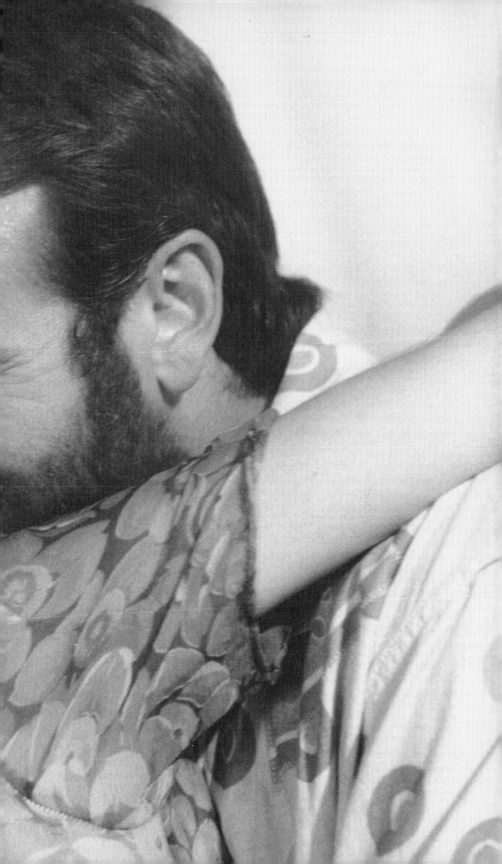

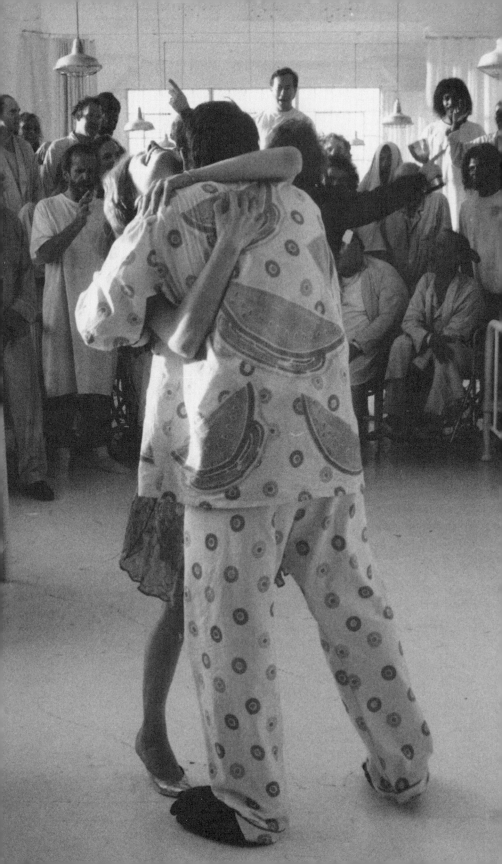

but CARMICHAEL remains unconscious. He reads the bottle:
Seconal. JACK looks at CARMICHAEL's limp body and checks his
heart. It is very faint. Scared, JACK slowly starts backing
out of the room.

                                                    CUT TO:

98   INT.   FIRST FLOOR HALLWAY — NIGHT

JACK is panicked. He wants to run away. He looks to the
front entrance and sees an alarm system indicated by a tiny
beam of light that sits a few inches above the floor.
Suddenly, JACK knows what he is going to do.

                                                    CUT TO:

99   EXT.   CARMICHAEL TOWN HOUSE — NIGHT

JACK exits out the front door, setting off a slight buzz
from the alarm. He checks to see that no one is around, then
quickly runs down the street.

                                                    CUT TO:

100 INT.   PARRY'S WARD — NIGHT

PARRY lies asleep in a sea of lime green and watermelons.
JACK places the "Grail" in PARRY's lifeless hands. He pulls
a chair up beside the bed and sits.

                         JACK
               Okay ... I did my side of the bargain
               ... You gonna wake up now?
                         (no response)
               Want to think about it a little more
               ...? Okay.

JACK props his feet up on PARRY's bed and settles in to
sleep.

                                                    CUT TO:

101 INT.   PARRY'S WARD — DAWN

CAMERA opens on a newspaper headline being read by an
ORDERLY: "ACCIDENTAL SUICIDE ATTEMPT THWARTED BY NIGHT
PROWLER ... Thief Didn't Know Anyone Was Home, Escapes Empty
Handed!" ... CAMERA PANS PAST several beds until it ARRIVES
at PARRY's. JACK is asleep in a chair beside him. CAMERA on
PARRY's hands as they gently come to life and grasp the
chalice. PARRY opens his eyes, raising the chalice to him.
He sees JACK sleeping beside him and smiles.

                         PARRY
                    (whispers)
               I had this dream, Jack.

JACK remains asleep.

                                                 (CONTINUED)

                              PARRY
                         (continuing)
               I was married. I was married to this
               beautiful woman ... and you were there,
               too.
                         (pause)
               I really miss her, Jack. Is that okay?
               Can I miss her now?

JACK, his eyes closed, only pretends to be asleep, but in
truth he hears every word. A tear rolls down his cheek.
PARRY extends one hand, placing it on JACK's shoulder while
cradling the chalice with the other.

                                                  CUT TO:

102   INT.   OAKBROOK INSTITUTE — DAY

LYDIA makes her way down the corridor, pushing her way
through the swinging doors into PARRY's ward. She is stopped
in her tracks by what she sees.

PARRY has gathered all the PATIENTS to the center of the
room, and is teaching them to sing "Groovin'." JACK is
watching. Although most are not getting it, all are having a
good time. When one of the PATIENTS turns to look at LYDIA,
PARRY turns as well. His face lights up as he says:

                              PARRY
               Hiya, sweetheart! Where you been?

LYDIA loses control and begins to cry through her smile.
PARRY approaches and wraps his arms around her.

                              PARRY
                         (continuing)
               Don't cry ... Hey ...

LYDIA throws her arms around him.

                              PARRY
                         (continuing)
               ...Are you my girl? ... Are you my
               girl ... ?

LYDIA sobs and nods on his shoulder. PARRY holds her
tighter.

                                                  CUT TO:

103   INT.   VIDEO SPOT — DAY

ANNE sits in her office, a cigarette dangling from her
mouth, going over receipts. There is a knock at the door. A
beat of silence. ANNE raises her head to discover JACK,
holding a bouquet of flowers. He smiles. ANNE looks shocked,

                                                  (CONTINUED)

then, pulls herself together. they both are frozen in silence.

> ANNE
> Well! What do you want me to do —
> applaud?

> JACK
> How have you been?

> ANNE
> (coldly)
> Terrific. Going on a lot of dates ...
> seeing lots of men ... lots of dates ...

JACK nods. He is uncharacteristically nervous.

> ANNE
> (sincere, vulnerable)
> Jack, please ... I'm having a bad month.
> I'm not up to this. What are you doing
> here?

He takes a breath, looks at ANNE and pushes the words out of him.

> JACK
> I love you.

For once ANNE is speechless. She slowly rises from behind her desk in a way that JACK takes a step back in fear. ANNE walks up to him. She has no intention of making this easy.

> ANNE
> Excuse me, I didn't get all that ...
> Would you run that by me again?

JACK is dying. He could hardly say it the first time.

> JACK
> I think ...
> (quickly corrects himself)
> I ... I realized ... I love you.

> ANNE
> Uh-huh ... you son of a bitch!

She hauls off and cracks him a slap across the face that stuns him — his knees give out, lowering him to the floor. She quickly grabs his face with her hands and plants a passionate kiss on his lips, that slowly causes him to rise back up. He drops the flowers and grabs her. She mounts his body and begins to undo his suit. They go at it with such passion, they both fall to the floor.

> ANNE (O.C.)
> Jesus. What rock hit YOU in the head?

(CONTINUED)

103   CONTINUED:

CAMERA pans out of the store and up to the day sky, then
pans down from the night sky, filled with billowy clouds set
against a midnight blue backdrop.

104   **EXT.   CENTRAL PARK — NIGHT**

CAMERA pans down PARRY and JACK lying naked, cloudbusting.

                    PARRY
          Beautiful night, huh?

                    JACK
          Yeah ... Hey they're moving ...
               (pause)
          Am I doing that?

                    THE END

The Search For The Holy Reel

by Richard LaGravenese

If I had ever had to pitch this movie, it might never have been made. I still can't come up with a one-line concept to describe it. Studio executives expect to be approached with a simple one-line pitch that sums up the thrust, passion and details of a movie that, although unproduced, is playing continuously inside a little theatre in your head. For example, "A Detroit cop comes to Beverly Hills to investigate the murder of a friend." If you can spit it out in one line, chances are it will appeal to a wide group of people without frightening their sensibilities or religious beliefs.

The Fisher King was a spec script, "spec" being Hollywoodese for "wing and a prayer." Instead of selling the idea, you sell the completed script, unadulterated by anyone else's neuroses but your own.

Before the "call from Hollywood" came, I wrote three completely different drafts with three completely different stories over a couple of years. Their only common denominators were Jack and Parry. I was technically working for Aaron Russo Entertainment, writing *Rude Awakening* — which was a terrific original story by Niel Levy, who asked me to co-write the screenplay with him. It was my first break into movies. Before that I was part of a comedy duo playing clubs and colleges; and before that an actor/writer with eyes for nothing but the theatre. In order to make some extra money during this period, I started writing monologues and selling them to fellow acting students. My acting teacher, Kate MacGregory Stewart, saw some promise and gave my name to Joan Michlin Silver, who was putting together an off-Broadway review called *A . . . My Name Is Alice*. I sold my first bit of writing to that show and I couldn't believe the ease with which it all happened. How much more confident I felt in front of a blank page instead of an audience. So I thought to hell with acting — let's ride the horse in the direction it wants to go.

Rude Awakening took three years of rewrites, the first two years of which I made a few thousand dollars. Unbelievable. But when you're eager to start your life, to work as a writer, there's only one reality that means anything to you and that's when a producer says, "I'm going to make this movie." This is the substance we lived on instead of a paycheck. It was a frustrating initiation to the biz. I was newly married. My wife was supporting us working in a video production house. I wanted my life to begin. I was spurred on to take action. I searched for an idea to a story all my own. Instead, I got an idea for two characters.

I went to the movies one night and, coming home, I saw a handsome young man walking with what appeared to be a mentally retarded young man. Their relationship — the way they walked together, side by side, across the street — sparked something. I fantasized about the loyalty and love between them. They seemed to have an inseparable bond made not out of blood, but out of choice, devotion and affection (such are the romantic visions of frustrated writers).

I then happened to read a psychology book by Robert Johnson called *He* in which the Fisher King, or Grail, myth — when paralleled with the male psyche — becomes the story of every man's psychological and spiritual growth. Johnson uses Jungian analysis to explain how a boy, at some specific turning point in his journey from innocence to adulthood, experiences a metaphysical awakening — either consciously or unconsciously. He senses within himself a divine connection to the world around him. He contacts a divinity within, a Godlike reflection — an "I can do anything in this world" kind of feeling. During a brief personal moment of mystical empowerment, the boy "touches" God or the God within — that part of ourselves that is our direct link to the divine; our souls. But being young boys, our innocence, eagerness and naïveté leave us unable to cope with or even understand the enormity of this experience — and so the experience burns us — leaving a "Fisher King" wound.

Parry's monologue in Central Park is a variation on the story Johnson tells. Both concern a young king out in the woods alone. Johnson's king touches a salmon he has cooking on the fire. Now, if you didn't know that the salmon/fish symbol represents the Christ energy or divinity within, you'd think he was just a moron who can't cook. I replaced the salmon with a vision of the Grail because it was a more accessible symbol.

However the wound is received, it is a wound men unconsciously seek to heal throughout their lives by acquiring a superficial sense of divine power — either with high paying jobs, fast cars, beautiful women or stardom (as in Jack Lucas's case). But since the wound is in the soul, these material accomplishments mean nothing. One must take the higher road — beyond the physical realities our minds impose and open up to higher realms of being and awareness. What really *is* important in life? Why does Jack feel, as he says to Parry, that even though he has everything he wants, he has nothing? There is a greater goal than just self-fulfillment, a greater power to be attained than material success and that is through service for the greater good or even someone you love. In this way we can truly reconnect with, or discover for the first time, our soul life — since it is the soul that is connected to all souls. So when we serve the one or the "all," we actually serve ourselves.

The Fisher King legend began to reverberate through my life, through my view of the world around me. The eighties were peaking. Narcissism was starting to consume itself, like a snake with its tail in its mouth. Through my own attempts at a spiritual awakening I began to understand all the destruction this global self-obsession was causing. Like a pendulum swinging back, the future's survival would rest on the ability of people to serve something beyond themselves, beyond their own individual needs.

So I decided to tell a story about a narcissistic man who, by the end of the movie, commits a completely selfless act. However, I still had no idea what form this story would take.

From Johnson's book, I learned that the only character who can take that first step on a soul journey is the fool. Only a simple-minded innocent will disregard the logic and dangers of reality and seek something invisible, imaginative or Godlike. I've always been intrigued by the logic of insanity, the beauty of it — how it seems to underscore all that we hold most dear — how perhaps insane people have a better handle on true reality than us so-called sane ones. The heroic, the artistic, the dreamers — all seem to have that crazy streak in them, as if their connection to something higher was too much for their human minds to contain.

I came up with Jack Lucas and Parry (Parsifal, the fool or young knight in the Grail Myth). Parry is, at first, the fool who will lead Jack on his soul's journey. As the movie progresses — especially in the third act — they switch roles; Parry becomes the wounded king and Jack must play the fool to steal the Grail that will save him. I hoped to convey that each man is both fool and wounded king. In other words, you don't need a Parry to find your higher self — he's already inside you. (There was a part of the Central Park monologue that concerned this but it was cut, the scene being a bit long to begin with.)

The first draft was a Kafka-esque tome in which Jack was an existential cab driver and Parry was an idiot savant. Jack used Parry's ability with numbers to win at casino (sound familiar?) Parry however, was more idiot than savant, and the feeling of the script was very *Of Mice and Men*. Changing him, I lost a little of the innocence that had originally attracted me to the character, but the script was unforgivably bleak. By the end, only Parry was saved — Jack remained a loser — alone and unfulfilled (real uplifting stuff! I was coming out of a mood that lasted ten years). But the bleakness was only one reason for abandoning this draft.

One dismal Friday I shall never forget, in the *New York Times* "At The Movies" column, a movie called *Rainman* was mentioned — about a fast talking man and his idiot savant brother. If it had been a thirties movie, the words IDIOT

SAVANT would have leapt off the page and zoomed into camera. My head whirled (I have this abnormal fear of being unoriginal). I raised my fist and cursed the collective unconscious — ruing the day I started meditating, which obviously left all my ideas vulnerable to writers on the other side of the country. I threw away my idiot savant Parry and searched for something else. As I've come to learn from these experiences, I could not have received a greater gift. I made a powerful discovery: there is always another idea.

Charlie Chaplin, in his autobiography, speaks of ideas and how to work with them. Mack Sennett remarked, "We have no scenario — we get an idea then follow the natural sequence of events." Chaplin himself said, " . . . pick a subject that will stimulate you, elaborate it and involve it, then, if you can't develop it further, discard it and pick another. Elimination from accumulation is the process of finding what you want." It's a difficult task for the ego to let an idea go, but that's only because there's a lack of faith that another idea will take its place. Be bold! When one is bold, one invites the Muses to participate.

The second draft of *Fisher King* was a sitcom. Jack will score an inheritance if he can marry off his dunce of a cousin Lydia to Parry, a simple-minded bum. I looked at old movies I loved and wanted to turn my story into something with more of a screwball quality. But it had no guts. (The best thing that came out of this draft was the character of Lydia.) Although there was a lot off funny stuff in there, I threw it all out and started over.

Some of William Goldman's best advice: sometimes you have to kill your little darlings in order to realize the script. But I still never knew where the story was going. Like Mack Sennett, I just followed the natural progression — I let each scene tell me where to go next. I tried writing outlines and index cards. But nothing worked as well as just getting in there and getting my hands dirty. I know screenwriting books tell you to work all this stuff out first but I found that if you're going for a truly original story, letting the script unfold allows for some unique creative directions — as long as you have your end goal in sight. So, I let the characters guide me to a story.

When I hit on the idea of Jack being a radio D.J. along the lines of a Howard Stern, everything fit into place (albeit over a year later). The nasty humor. The callousness and irresponsibility to the adoring public. It all fit well with Jack's ruthlessness to get ahead. Then, when I connected Parry's wife to the tragedy, everything just explained itself. Parry became an ordinary man who was the victim of extraordinary circumstances. A lot of possibilities opened up for me now — especially in contrasting Parry to Jack, the man whose heart has for years been an ignored organ. Parry, or Henry Sagan, was all heart. A man in love, whose love exploded before his eyes.

The idea of a lonely, faceless man, Edwin Malnick, coming into our lives from nowhere and destroying what we hold most dear becomes frightenly more real as one shocking newspaper headline replaces the next. There are so many disconnected people looking for connections. Parry could be any of us — victimized by fate, yet heroic enough to survive and continue his own way.

Jack becomes a man caught between what he wants and the truth of what he wants. He knows stardom is bullshit, but he wants it more than anything. He can't seem to reconcile these two truths. Originally, Jack was more angry, more paranoid about the world. His radio show was propelled by his anger, with monologues about the Bernard Goetz trial and the insanity of the streets prompting a more forceful public reaction. At Disney, Jack went from Howard Stern to David Letterman — more cynical; not as socially outraged.

There was originally much more paranoia in Jack. He started out being more fatalistic. In the limo with his agent, he exhibited a sense of doom about his future. Even if he got the sitcom, "What does it all mean?" But he was too self-aware in these opening moments; the audience would be ahead of the movie. The story would be better if he, and the audience, were shocked into this awareness — taken by complete surprise.

Once these ideas were in place, the script took a few months to complete. It was an odd script. I really didn't have a lot of faith in it ever being produced. Only my wife Ann kept believing that there was an actual, producible movie there. I thought at best it would be a writing sample which might lead to other work. When I did allow myself the occasional fantasy of it being produced, it was always with some independent production company and a cast of unknowns. I honestly never dreamt it would be realized at the level at which it was made.

I had just joined with ICM through Jeremy Zimmer, who was a good friend of Ann's. He in turn assigned me to Steve Rabineau. As luck would have it, this was smack dab in the middle of the longest writers' strike in history. No one could buy anything. My life was still on hold. So, we waited. And waited. And waited. My wife kept the faith. I tried to keep my sense of humor. But the strike lingered on.

Finally the strike ended. My agent was allowed to submit the script; we heard nothing for weeks. We decided we deserved a vacation and took an inexpensive trip to Puerto Rico. I figured, to hell with it — whatever happens, happens. I had done my work. Now it was up to the Gods.

The Gods have an interesting sense of humor. During the weekend we were away, *everything* happened. When we came home late Monday night, there were eighteen messages on our answering machine: producers and agents. "Where are you?" was the popular question.

Rabineau had submitted the script to Hill/Obst Productions via Stacey Sher, who was their assistant at the time. She in turn gave it to Lynda Obst who, with Debra Hill, had a production deal at Disney. Hill/Obst were in the process of finishing up *Heartbreak Hotel* for Disney when they submitted the script to exec Jane Goldenring to see if Disney would buy it for them. Twenty minutes into Jane's pitch, Jeffrey Katzenberg stopped her and said, "Jane, what's it about?" She proceeded to take off her shoes and bang the table with them in a valiant attempt to explain that, although the script might be slightly off-center, it was worth Disney's involvement. Jane succeeded in her pitch to Katzenberg, and this led to a three-picture deal at Disney Studios — *Fisher King* plus two others to be chosen at a later date. (Those two scripts are still in development.)

Before the Disney deal, there was a brief period when Columbia wanted to buy *The Fisher King* for Richard Pryor. They offered twice Disney's price. This was my first major league decision, since even my agents couldn't honestly advise me to say no. And then Aaron Russo wanted to buy it, feeling that I was disloyal by not showing it to him first. He, too, was offering more money.

But I knew that Lynda, Debra and Stacey understood the movie. I knew they would attempt to keep it as close to the "movie in my mind" as possible. I also knew the Richard Pryor idea was wrong. I went with Disney.

Disney had it for five months, during which I gave them everything they asked for in terms of rewrites — I was so grateful to be earning a living. But the script was protected by its own strangeness. It wasn't open to a lot of interpretation — you either had to go with it or completely change it. At first, Disney wanted to try and make it more mainstream. Their most salient objective was to make the stealing of the Holy Grail what they call a "set piece" (sort of like a show-stopping number in a musical).

They suggested I watch *Topkapi*, which worried me. I wrote a scene in which Jack rollerskated through a museum filled with laser beams. We all hated it, but again, the prospect of "getting the movie made" was starting to obsess us.

BEWARE! It's like a drug. The lessons I learned with Aaron were quickly being forgotten. Luckily, the Gods intervened later on.

Disney also wanted a lot of the "bum stuff" shortened or deleted. They felt it was too dark. Lynda Obst was especially skilled at receiving copious and detailed instructions from the studio and helping me translate them into scenes that maintained and sometimes improved the script. This was especially true for the character of Anne.

"Anne" is a real woman who runs a real video store on Second Avenue, where my wife and I first lived. She's a real doll — every time we'd come in, she'd come out from behind the counter and give us hugs and kisses like we were family. She reminded me of my own Italian mother and aunts.

Later I wanted very much to curb Anne's Italian persona because it had recently been done to death in *Moonstruck, Married To The Mob*, etc. I was particularly concerned because Mercedes Ruehl, who plays Anne in our movie, had played a similar role in *Married to the Mob*. Fortunately, Mercedes — an incredibly intelligent actress — felt the same way, and Anne came alive through her performance in a way I had always fantasized. Mercedes' earthiness, honesty, humor — and her ability to expose this ferocious rage of a wounded heart — made me think I'd written it for her. During the filming of her big "It's over!" scene with Jack, every man on the set cringed with discomfort as she nailed him.

During script development at Disney, Anne's character was expanded. The scene in which she and Jack break up, for example, was written during this time. Originally, I cut to the third act with Jack back to his asshole self. The idea of helping Parry get together with Lydia by using Jack's radio techniques (the scene on the phone with Lydia; use of the tape recorded song) was also a Disney through line. Disney made their requests, but thanks to Lynda, Stacey and Debra, I was able to incorporate them into the script my way. Which is probably why after all these changes were completed, Disney put the project into turnaround. (Turnaround is when a studio resells a script they've optioned, including costs they've incurred since they bought it.) I don't think as a writer you ever know the real reasons for something like that. I was told it just wasn't something Disney, or Katzenberg, was interested in making.

Disney had turned my movie into something they didn't like as much as the original they had bought; but now they didn't want to make the original either. Go figure. They did love the writing, however, and my two-picture deal remained intact. Katzenberg very graciously put it into turnaround quickly, something for which I shall always be grateful. With ICM's help the movie moved with ease over to Tri-Star Pictures. Tri-Star executive Steve Randall told me they had originally wanted to buy it back when Disney first optioned me. I'm convinced it wound up at the place it was meant to be, in spite of all manner of worrying and anxiety. There is a perfect order — even in Hollywood.

Disney's notes were a valiant attempt to make the film something it wasn't — lighter, funnier, more action packed. Why did they buy it in the first place? Well, something about its initial attraction had to do with the writers' strike.

A Disney executive told me that after the strike was over, the industry expected a lot of highly original work — given the extended opportunity for writers to write for themselves. (He also asked me if I wrote *Fisher King* on acid.)

Apparently many writers actually used the time to turn out more cop movies or products they thought would sell. There are successful screenwriters who try to monitor what the marketplace is looking for and source their material from that perspective. The writers who make a mark on the industry — who have something to really contribute — points of views and ideas that Hollywood doesn't know it's looking for until it sees them — these to me are the inspirations, the lifeblood of the industry.

Finding a director was a challenge. We had a period of five months during which James Cameron had expressed interest. He was tempted to switch genres and try more of a character piece, but he couldn't decide during the making of *The Abyss* so ICM (who represented Cameron, my producers and me) took the script off the market for five months until he finished that film and was ready to make a decision. After five months, he said no. We were back where we started.

The people over at CAA were also keen on the script and, thanks to them, it made its way to Terry Gilliam, Robin Williams and Jeff Bridges. Suddenly the movie I thought would be a low budget art movie was becoming a major package.

In Robert Bly's book *Iron John*, he speaks of the Wild Man in each of us — the spontaneous, the intuitive, the bold. It has nothing to do with machismo or savagery. It is about man claiming his unconscious spirit in order to fly. Bly speaks of initiation of young men by older men — of the responsibility the older man has to bless the younger man, who desperately needs this acknowledgment in order to find his way in becoming whole. In the fable, the Wild Man takes the boy on his shoulders into the woods, away from mother and father, and towards his destiny. Terry was my Wild Man.

Up until this point, my main objective in life was to be liked. I had sort of a Willy Loman psychosis going on. I was the perennial good boy who was to have the notorious bad boy of movies direct my script. When I heard they had sent it to Terry, I was honored, but I knew he never did anyone else's material so I didn't think he'd be interested. Lucky for me, the timing was perfect, and all that worrying about writers' strikes and James Cameron and time lost was for nothing. The right director found it at the right time. Perfect order.

When I heard he wanted to do it, I flipped. I, like so many others in New York, were among the first in line when *Brazil* played on the East Side for just a week, during that big Universal controversy. Terry, on his own or with the Python troupe, represented the smartest, boldest and silliest comedy could get. They were idols of mine, ever since they first hit the States on Sunday nights at 10:30 on public television. Having Terry direct this script was, to my mind, like getting Shane to protect the ranch. There was no way it could get fucked up. It could be as unique a story as it wanted. It could only get better.

Terry told me that in each of his movies he always identified with his main character. The trouble with *Fisher King* , he said, was that he identified with both Jack and Parry. I thought that was great news! We sat on the floor of his hotel room and went over the script page by page. As we did, we noticed that several things had gotten lost during the post-Disney collation. And this is another worthwhile point: By the time it went into turnaround, two drafts of the film had been written. Lynda guided a "best of the two" version, with scenes from each. Naturally, a lot of material got lost during this process as well.

If you've already covered the "information," according to a common Hollywood attitude, you can cut whatever seems repetitious. Now, I'm not advocating repetition, but a movie isn't just about giving information — it's about setting a mood and painting three-dimensional, surprising characters. It's also a house of cards. Little edits here can create giant termite holes over there; or a scene just doesn't play as well, usually because a of minor change.

When Parry stands on Anne's kitchen table and sings "Holdin' My Penis," originally the joke was set up by stage directions explaining that the only reason Parry was asking for more food was to get a glimpse at Anne's cleavage. It had been years since he was that close to a beautiful, voluptuous female. This direction had been cut, having been deemed unnecessary exposition and, at the time, ever-grateful me couldn't explain why it was important. Once I showed Terry the original setup, the scene came alive for him.

The character of Sid, the crippled vet in Grand Central Station (played perfectly by Tom Waits) was a major bone of contention. "Why do we need him?" "He doesn't advance the plot." "It's too long." This debate lasted all the way through preview screenings after the movie was completed. Terry was a firm supporter of Sid — he added a flavor, a tone, and his scene remains one of the most memorable moments in the movie.

Terry had me put back many scenes and descriptions lost during the post-Disney collation. He understood the darkness of the script and wanted more of it. I was thrilled. I was always afraid of the script falling into sentimentality. As a writer, it's one of my Achilles' heels (I have several). I can get sappy real easily. I sometimes dream of writing the ultimate Bette Davis movie. I gave Terry the draft that was originally bought and, in a way, felt more validated than when it was first sold.

What Terry wanted to cut I found surprising at first. Originally, when Jack was on his descent into hell leading to his suicide attempt in Act One, he had become such a misanthrope and so paranoid that he, too, had hallucinations.

I had thought at first that this gave him a connection to Parry's world — they had something in common. But Terry wanted to keep things simple. He felt it was too "Gilliamesque." When Jack goes after the Grail in Act Three, the use of hallucinations works more poignantly than if we had seen it earlier as well. It is as if Jack truly has to step into Parry's world in order to save him. Another hallucination in that robbery sequence was filmed but got cut. It is included in the selection of deleted scenes.

Originally, there were a couple of more radio bits and I'd given Jack more of a relationship with the two techies that work in the booth. I worried about the audience really understanding who Jack was, so I overwrote. Terry cut me down. He came up with the idea of having the phrase that Jack repeats in the bathtub (as he memorizes his lines) be sort of a pop mantra that gets absorbed into the culture, the way lines from *Saturday Night Live* used to. Originally, Jack repeated "I want my orange cup with the teddy bear." After Terry's note I came up with "Forgive me" — which we also gave to the woman in the video store and the cab driver that almost runs him over outside of Anne's apartment. So no matter where Jack went, he was haunted by his failure. Terry also felt very strongly about actually *seeing* the murder of Parry's wife. He felt that to believe Parry's state of mind, the audience had to experience the same horror and shock.

The rewrites continued pretty much through most of the New York filming. Jack's Nietzsche speech was originally in a bar spoken to a bartender, but budget limitations made it a soliloquy under a statue. Time cuts required that the beginning of Act Three be shortened. There was much more material showing that Jack had returned to his former self before his decision to visit the catatonic Parry. Also, he discovered, as he retraced his steps to find Parry, that one of the bums from his rescue in Act One, the youngest, was found dead. This was actually an idea that came up during pre-production and was filmed, then cut. Parry's through line as a modern day Don Quixote was likewise severely cut.

Terry included me in aspects of filmmaking that writers are not often privy to; I was involved with rehearsals, I worked on the set, attended dailies, sat in on marketing meetings as well as powwows with studio people. Terry set up an atmosphere of such respect and creative exchange that no one person seemed to dominate. He once told me his job was to field the creative ideas from his crew, then pick and choose which he thought best. Everyone was invited to dailies; if they worked on the film, he felt they deserved to be there. I started to feel that I could at least communicate my opinions, whether they had an effect or not. I don't think I would have dared if the director had been anyone else.

The filming began in New York — all exteriors, except for one backup interior. Most of these were night scenes. The cast — Robin, Jeff, Mercedes and Amanda Plummer — was set. Rehearsals began and suddenly the script came to life. My next set of rewrites came out of ideas created in this first week of rehearsals.

Robin asked for old drafts to look through for lines that might have been lost as well as different versions of the Fisher King monologue in Central Park (there were at least half a dozen). This monologue became a real community effort, as everyone had an idea about what it meant, or what it should mean. In the set one day, I even got a call from two Los Angeles location people I'd never met, asking why I had cut certain lines from the version they'd read. They then sent me a tape recorded version of the Grail Myth.

Terry loved the idea of stopping the movie, and the frenzy of Parry, to just sit down and tell a story. His knowledge of the myth was based on how the wound of the king was connected to the land — how the kingdom itself would die in direct relation to the king's physical health. I was more interested in the psychological interpretations. Robin and Jeff both had individual lines and concepts from old drafts that they thought were important. But the monologue was getting too long (even though I love monologues). Finally Terry, Jeff, Robin, his wife Marsha and I sat down for dinner and went over all the different versions. After each of the men pitched his desired interpretation, it was Marsha who reminded us that we should tell the simplest story and let the audience find their own meaning. With Robin's help, I put together what sounded coherent and would be the simplest to play. The version in the movie is actually somewhat edited from what was actually filmed. It's amazing to discover how little you need on screen. It was all there anyway.

One idea that came directly out of rehearsals was the staging of the scene in which Jack brings Parry back to the apartment as part of the "coincidental" first meeting of Parry and Lydia. Although most of the dialogue is the same as originally written, the staging — Parry remaining in the doorway wanting to leave and the two couples, Anne/Lydia and Parry/Jack, whispering furiously to one another — came out of rehearsal. The scene in which Jack and Anne watch a sitcom, when Jack has his "I'm glad I'm not famous" speech, was half constructed on the set. Mercedes and I sat together and threw lines back and forth for "Anne" that felt more in keeping with the character in that moment. With her help, Anne's role in the scene was better than originally conceived.

All the actors had a hand in evolving the characters, and each in a completely different way.

Robin's skill at ad-libbing is unequaled and it was always welcome; but he was also very respectful of the script. For example, his entrance under the

133

bridge was a difficult scene for me to write. I never thought it was funny and I was secretly hoping Robin could improve it. He wound up doing several versions, adding his own ideas both during filming and later in dubbing sessions. He also gave me the idea of looking through *Don Quixote* and Dante's *Inferno* for quotes that Parry could mutter spontaneously, as he does when he hears the cry of the gay bum in the park.

Robin's genius fit Parry's insanity like a glove. His ability to go off on a thousand creative tangents infused Parry with an electrically charged sense of awe, as if he had a nonstop fireworks display going on inside his head. And when he stops to take off the fool's mask, it breaks your heart.

He also inspired the filming itself. I remember one night in particular, filming the Chinese restaurant scene. It was about five in the morning, and we'd been there since seven the night before. Everyone's energy was drained. Suddenly Robin did twenty minutes of nonstop impersonations and comedy. I remember one of the grips turning to me with tears in his eyes, he was laughing so hard. Everyone was rejuvenated and juiced. Then Terry turned to me and said, "Thank God for him."

And thank God for Jeff Bridges. If Robin was the Ariel spirit that took flight, Jeff was the foundation upon which to build. The first night we met for dinner and pored over every page as Jeff asked questions and came up with ideas on how to play each line. He's amazing. His skill is so seamless, you don't see all the work — you just see this raw character who can flip from ice coldness to complete and vulnerable despair. Terry and I were continually blown away by what he could produce. On the set, Jeff was so aware of every aspect — from lighting, to how a simple facial gesture would read in the frame, to how much volume to bring to a certain phrase. He came up with ideas for other actors as well, but always with tremendous care and respect. It was Jeff's idea to make a tiny chair out of a champagne cork, which Parry offers to Lydia as a gift during their walk to the restaurant. It became one of the loveliest moments in the movie for me.

Terry cast Amanda Plummer because he wanted a Lydia who appeared to be from another time — as if what Parry saw in her stemmed from his own background in medieval history. Lydia was a schlub to everyone else, but to Parry she was a damsel in distress. I remember Amanda in rehearsals. The first few days she just mumbled the lines, took huge pauses — as if she wouldn't say anything that wasn't absolutely felt. Then, near the end of the week, suddenly she just became Lydia. There was no line between them. She had birthed this character from the inside and created this incandescence that *was* Lydia. Her scenes with Mercedes, who also comes from a theatre background, were some of the greatest spectator times for me.

I never wrote the waltz scene in Grand Central Station. Terry simply threw out the idea after seeing the main rotunda. The scene captured the essence of that moment in the script, but with much more magic and beauty. I had written that after Sid gives his monologue to Jack, a black bag woman begins to sing *a capella*. Jack sits and watches as people stop in their busy day to listen and he begins to feel a sense of community and ease. Suddenly the room is transformed for him. At the same time, Parry follows Lydia, but the music he hears in his head is classical and rapturous. After it's over the two reunite and both comment on what a beautiful song they heard, each not knowing the other heard a different song. It was a moment when we saw Jack beginning to step into Parry's world vision. Although Jack's moment in this scene was a little lost, the idea of the waltz transported the audience, instead of Jack, into Parry's world. And I think the effect was tremendous. In order for us to believe that Parry worships this woman, we need to penetrate his fantasy, and the effect of the image lasts throughout the film.

Terry is visual. I'm much more literal. My favorite movies are strongly scripted with emphasis on character. We crossed our bridges to meet at the center, which is why the film has an interesting combination of styles. I did learn, however, that if you want to write a heavily scripted movie — what I think of as a movie for actors — you've got to learn to be concise within the writing or you'll lose a lot of what you feel is important.

The scene under the bridge where Jack drinks with Parry's bum squad was one of the first scenes I ever wrote and lasted through every version of the script. My intention was to emulate those Preston Sturges scripts in which even small, tertiary characters have moments that remain in your mind. They don't need grand development — they just enter the story for a brief moment, have their bit and leave. In a flash you encounter a three-dimensional character that leaves behind a little wisdom. (Sturges' favorites seemed to be bartenders.)

Well, it didn't work out that way. The location was so overwhelming that the scene became more about the visual; the characters became visuals within the visual. But if Terry had filmed everything the way it was intended, the movie would have become a mini-series.

I tend to write a lot of dialogue. I like actors to have lines to act. I get excited by performances. I also give a lot of subtextual direction with the lines — emotional clues. More often than not actors ignore these directions, but at least as a writer I have the freedom to get a little more intricate in the dialogue by not only scoring the interplay of lines, but the interplay of subtext. I can have a character react not simply off another line, but off the subtext he senses.

Another advantage to being concise is that you get so many ideas on the set, so many little inspirations, that you may want to leave the script open in certain areas so you have room to add (like the waltz scene). Either way, the process is give and take. You must choose your battles wisely or else you become a force that is resisting the horse in the direction it's heading.

I'm glad I spoke up in the case of one scene. When Jack and Anne are watching the sitcom, Jack insults Anne deeply and she leaves terribly hurt. When the actors first came on the set, they played scenes how they saw them — which more often than not gave Terry the angles with which to shoot. However, in this instance, the actors staged it so that Anne stays rooted and Jack walks all around the room, ultimately getting angry and exiting. I told Terry that was not the way the scene really worked, and I mentioned my stage directions which described Jack remaining glued to the television set except for a brief moment when he refills his drink. Anne tries to carry on a meaningful conversation but Jack's obsession is clearly with the sitcom. After he insults Anne without even looking at her, she exits — and we are left alone with him and the sitcom as we repeat the phrase "Forgive me!" and Jack mumbles under his breath, "Madness.). Terry joked that at this point in the fifty-day shooting schedule, neither he nor anyone else had read the script for some time. He then made a funny announcement that the author wanted the scene to be played as written. Everyone laughed and no one had any problems with playing it according to the script.

Throughout all the drafts and studios, once a film gets underway, something funny happens. People who have been associated with the movie at one point in the past will meet you and congratulate you on the production. Then, invariably, they will mention their favorite part of the script that they "hope is still in the movie." Of course, it isn't. And you must face their disappointment, chin up, resigned that they will hate the movie when it opens.

A common cry in Hollywood is, "Oh, it was a much better script." — as if, no matter what movie they see, they've already read the book. Usually, the book IS better, but reading a book is a private activity wherein you can conjure up your own images and sensations. For many studio people and producers this happens with scripts. They can't help but imagine how it all becomes real. But transforming a script from a page-turner to a reel-changer is a collaborative process. That's what makes it exciting. Coming from a theatrical background (albeit non-professional), the most rewarding moments I can remember were not in performance, but in the magic of creative exchange and interplay. Until I direct myself, I value this kind of respect between director and writer, writer and cast, etc. . . . (Although people tell me it will never happen again).

In a way, the script acted as its own Grail for me — healing wounds of self-doubt, when years ago I first put my hand in the fire and dreampt of glory. I am grateful for everyone associated with its realization. Now, as always, it is up to those ". . . wonderful people in the dark . . ." (Wilder/Diamond, *Sunset Boulevard*) to let us know if the story was worth telling.

A Selection of Deleted and Altered Scenes

*"All in all . . . the movie is most faithful to the script. This is
proven by the fact that, even now watching it in a theater, I still
can't explain it to anyone in one sentence."*

—Richard LaGravenese

JACK'S ORIGINAL RADIO INTRO; JACK TORTURES EDWIN

This was Jack's first radio broadcast, which sparked the Edwin Malnick
tragedy. The script called for many different sound effects strengthening the
idea of Edwin being humiliated by Jack and his crew. It emphasized the
interplay of Jack and his crew, which immediately switched to hostility once
the broadcast was over.

```
INT.    DARKENED ROOM — DAWN

C.U. — A RADIO/ALARM CLOCK reads 5:59 AM. The digital
numbers flip to 6:00 and the radio goes on:

A TALK SHOW HOST speaks in a soft, soothing voice:

                JACK (V.O.)
        It's six a.m. ... Oooooooo and that bed
        never felt soooo good ... Mmmmmmm, you
        linger in a gentle dream state ... ever
        so comfortable ... ever so safe ...

SOUND EFFECTS — LOUD BATTLE NOISE . . .

                JACK
            (continuing)
        ... BUT SUDDENLY YOU REALIZE IT'S
        MONDAY!

A WOMAN SCREAMS ... THE D.J., JACK, speaks in a rapid fire
pace ...

A HAND from O.C. tries to shut the alarm off in the dark.

                JACK
            (continuing)
        ... your hand races to shut off the
        alarm before your mind wakes up ...

SCREAMS ... THE HAND knocks over a water glass and grabs the
clock but can't find the off switch.

                                    (CONTINUED)
```

139

> JACK
> (continuing)
> ... But it's too late! If you don't get
> out of bed now, you'll never have enough
> time to blow dry your hair THAT SPECIAL
> WAY ... You'll never make that nine
> o'clock meeting that your PARTNER WILL
> BE EARLY FOR ... YOU'LL BE LATE AND
> EVERYONE WILL NOTICE!

THE HAND bangs the clock violently ...

> JACK
> (continuing)
> ... Rumors will fly about you losing
> your edge and before you know it, you're
> selling yourself on street corners to
> lonely middle-aged men from the Midwest
> ... Headlines flash across your mind —
> SLEEPER GUNS D.J. THEN SELF — CLAIMED "I
> only wanted two more minutes!"

SCREAMS ... SILENCE ... The D.J. (JACK) speaks in a normal
voice.

> JACK
> (continuing)
> ... Hey, it's Monday morning, and I'm
> Jack Lucas.

THE HAND rips the clock off the night table.

> CALLER (V.O.)
> Hello Jack, it's Edwin.

> JACK AND CREW (V.O.)
> IT'S EDWIN!!!!

New Years Eve sound effects.

> JACK (V.O.)
> Edwin. We haven't heard from you in a
> while. I've missed you.

> EDWIN (V.O.)
> (laughing good-naturedly)
> O.K. ... O.K. ...
> (sincere, child-like)
> I missed you too, Jack.

> JACK AND CREW (V.O.)
> Awwww.......!!!!

SOUND EFFECTS — "A SUMMER PLACE" ... THE NEEDLE IS SCRATCHED
OFF.

EDWIN laughs, perhaps a bit overzealously — He is a simple
minded soul ... a lonely child in the body of a lonely man.

(CONTINUED)

> JACK (V.O.)
> So, Edwin baby, this is Sunrise
> Confession time ... what have you got
> for us?

> EDWIN (V.O.)
> I ... I ... went to this bar ... this
> very, you know, IN place ... called The
> Side Bar.

> JACK (V.O.)
> I know the place. It's one of those
> YUPPIE gathering holes. I told you to
> stay away from them, Edwin. Yuppies are
> diseased individuals who went to private
> schools and took scouting seriously.

> EDWIN (V.O.)
> (simple-minded laughter)
> O.K. I know, but ... I met this
> beautiful girl ...

SOUND EFFECT — "WEDDING BELLS" THEN A NEEDLE SCRATCHING IT
OFF.

> JACK (V.O.)
> Now, Edwin, I'm going to have to
> remind you of the time we made you
> propose to that check-out girl at
> Thrifty's that you liked so much.
> Remember her reaction?

> BLACK SEVENTIES GROUP (V.O.)
> "MISTER BIG STUFF ... HUH ... TELL ME
> ... WHO DO YOU THINK YOU ARE ...
> MISTER BIG STUFF ... YOU'RE NEVER
> GOING TO GET MY LOVE ..."

> EDWIN (V.O.)
> (defensive)
> I wasn't really serious about her,
> Jack. That was just a joke for you
> guys ... She was just a girl. This is
> a woman. She wears pearls.

> JACK AND CREW (V.O.)
> Aahhh.

> EDWIN (V.O.)
> I think she likes me ... she gave me
> her number, but she must work a lot
> 'cause when I call she's never home
> ... But I think we'll go out this
> weekend ... I've —

> JACK (V.O.)
> Yeah, Edwin, SURE ... and PINNOCHIO
> is a true story ... EDWIN! WAKE UP!
> This is ANOTHER fairy tale.

(CONTINUED)

CONTINUED:

                        EDWIN (V.O.)
          No, Jack, it's not.

                        JACK (V.O.)
          She gave you the brush off, kiddo. How
          long ago did you meet?

                        EDWIN (V.O.)
          Um ... I think it's like two weeks
          almost.

                        JACK (V.O.)
          TWO WEEKS? And she's never home? What,
          does she commute to Saigon every day?
          Edwin, please ...

                        EDWIN (V.O.)
                  (hurt)
          JACK! She LIKES me. She said for me to
          call.

                        MICHAEL MCDONALD (V.O.)
                  (sings)
          "WHAT A FOOL BELIEVES ... HE SEES ..."

                        EDWIN (V.O.)
                  (over the song)
          JACK!

                        JACK (V.O.)
          I told you about those kind of people,
          Edwin. They only mate with their own
          kind. It's called YUPPIE IN-BREEDING —
          that's why so many of them are retarded
          and wear the same clothes. You are not
          their kind, Edwin ... They're not human.
          They're evil, Edwin

SLIGHT PAUSE, as EDWIN considers this.

                        EDWIN (V.O.)
                  (serious)
          O.K., Jack.

END CREDITS

                                                    CUT TO:

INT.   RADIO STATION — 9:30 A.M.

CAMERA PANS from a wall clock as JACK LUCAS winds up his
broadcast.

                        JACK LUCAS (V.O.)
          Well, I'm gone. I'm outta here. It's
          been a thrill, as always.
                  (MORE)

                                                (CONTINUED)

142

>   JACK (CONTINUED)
>   (false sincerity)
>   "Have a perfect day" ... and remember,
>   bosses are just cruel third graders who
>   have grown up and only pretended to be
>   mature so they could get jobs and be
>   cruel for money.

WE PAN several studio TECHNICIANS making ready for the end
of the broadcast to the talk show host JACK LUCAS —
handsome, aggressive, intelligent — an underground media
star.

>   JACK
>   Everyone here on the Jack Lucas Morning
>   Show says bye.

>   CREW
>   BYE!

THANKS FOR THE MEMORY plays.

>   JACK
>   This is Jack Lucas ... So long ...
>   arriverderch ... I'll be sure to send
>   you a thought as you struggle through
>   yet another eternal nine-to-fiver
>   ...Yes, I will — as I drive home in my
>   limo ... lay out on my sun deck ... have
>   sex with the teenager of my choice ...
>   And that thought will be: Thank God I'm
>   me!

JACK motions to a TECHY behind glass. Then leans back in his
chair, as a RADIO COMMERCIAL begins. His expression seems
grave — not one you would expect after a successful
broadcast. He appears tired and annoyed. He sighs in relief
that it is over. The STUDIO TEAM works around him in silence
— with no indication of the relationship they have "on air."
JACK pulls out a bottle of aspirins and takes two.

>   JACK
>   (annoyed, to the room)
>   I want you all to know I'm getting sick
>   again and it's because someone keeps
>   forgetting to raise the thermostat
>   before I come in here ... my ass is
>   freezing for the first hour.

A TECHY makes a mocking face behind his back. ANOTHER TECHY
suppresses a laugh.

CENTRAL PARK: PARRY LAYS TRAPS FOR DRUG DEALERS

Of the deleted scenes I've included, this one is an example of things lost along the way as more and more people get on board and claim a certain amount of territoriality. Initially, Parry was more of a Don Quixote character — cleaning up the streets with a good-natured Medieval vigilantism. In Central Park, Parry, with Jack's help, was originally laying a homemade trap to catch drug dealers: a net affixed to a tree with a device that would spring the trap with a slingshot and a rock.

When the first assistant director came on board, this was one of his cut suggestions. Terry agreed because he felt it was a little far out and, as I was reminded, Terry wanted to stay clear of things that seemed too Gilliamesque.

But I often think how including this aspect of Parry's character would have worked — his heroism in the face of personal misfortune.

EXT.   CENTRAL PARK'S GREAT LAWN — SAME NIGHT

JACK is helping PARRY lay out nets beneath an oak tree.

> PARRY
> This is a very popular tree with the
> crack dealers.

> JACK
> What I don't understand is — so you
> catch them in a net — what good is that?
> They don't go to jail.

> PARRY
> Jails are crowded. The way I think is
> ... if you can just ... annoy them on a
> regular basis ... let them know there
> are forces out there that are going to
> stop them — forces they can't see or
> even fight ... maybe, eventually,
> they'll give up and the Red Knight won't
> be able to use them.

JACK was following this philosophy with great interest until the mention of the Red Knight.

> JACK
> (cutting him off)
> Yeah, yeah, yeah ... right — but, why
> ... not just go after Carmichael. I
> mean, call the newpapers — put some
> pressure on him to fork up the uh ... ya
> know ... the cup.

PARRY changes the subject.

(CONTINUED)

                         PARRY
             What a beautiful night.

HE walks deeper into the open field. This makes JACK
nervous.

                         JACK
             Don't you think we should be getting out
             of here — it's getting late ...

PARRY starts to take off his clothes.

                         JACK
             ... What are you doing?

                         PARRY
             Have you ever done any cloudbusting?
             See, you take your clothes off, you lie
             on your back and you concentrate on
             staring at the clouds ... and you try to
             break them apart with your mind. It's
             wild.

He is now naked. He lies down.

                         JACK
             Parry, you can't do this. It's
             dangerous.

                         PARRY
             Well, that's stupid. This is my park
             just as much as it is theirs. You think
             it's fair they keep us out just because
             they make us think we'll get killed or
             something?

                         JACK
             Yes. I think that's very fair.

                         PARRY
             Come on, try it. Ya feel the air on your
             body — ya little fella's flappin' in the
             breeze ... everybody in the city is busy
             with their business and no one knows
             we're bare assed in the middle of it.
             Come on!

                         JACK
             NO! I'm leaving! I mean it ... this is
             nuts.
                     (walking O.C.)
             You're going to get yourself killed. I'm
             leaving. I mean it!

JACK starts walking away from PARRY, talking to himself —

                                        (CONTINUED)

                            145

CONTINUED:

                              JACK
                         (continuing)
          ... Ha ... little fella? I mean, what do
          I expect? The man talks to invisible
          people — he sees invisible horses — and
          he's naked in the middle of Central
          Park. I should be surprised. I'm fucking
          out of my mind to even be here!
                         (turns back and yells)
          YOU'RE OUT OF YOUR FUCKING MIND!!

HE walks O.C.

                                                    CUT TO:

EXT.   GREAT LAWN — TEN MINUTES LATER

JACK, naked, is lying next to PARRY looking up at the
clouds.

                              JACK
          They're not moving.

                              PARRY
          Sshhh.

THEY stare up. JACK raises his head.

                              JACK
          You sure no one's coming?

                              PARRY
          Why do you care?

                              JACK
          I don't know how I would explain this.
          "JACK LUCAS FOUND DEAD — NAKED — BESIDE
          ANOTHER DEAD, NAKED MAN ... THE TWO WERE
          DEAD ... AND NAKED" ... It'll probably
          boost my biography sales. People have a
          fascination for murdered naked
          celebrities.

                              PARRY
          You're a celebrity?

JACK realizes his opportunity. HE faces PARRY.

                              JACK
          Listen ... it was a little over a year
          ago ... Something happened ... I was
          responsible for —

                              PARRY
          Man, you are wound up so tight, Jack.
          You oughta relax a bit. I venture to say
          if I stuck a coil up your ass I could
          toast marshmallows.

                                              (CONTINUED)

                              146

                        JACK
                  (heartfelt)
          How do you do it? How do you get through
          every day the way you do?
                  (beat)

                        PARRY
          Did you ever hear the story of the
          Fisher King?

JACK shakes his head. CAMERA focuses on PARRY.

                        PARRY
          It's all about this king who lived in
          the castle where the Holy Grail was
          kept. Now this king was a good man, but
          he'd been through some awful times —
          tragedies, betrayals, disappointments,
          abandonment ... So much so, that the
          older he ... got, the more bitter about
          life he became ...

                                              CUT TO:

JACK listening ...

                        PARRY
                  (continuing)
          ... He had no faith in any man. No trust
          in himself ... he could no longer truly
          love, or feel loved — and so he started
          to die.

                                          CUT BACK TO:

PARRY ...

                        PARRY
                  (continuing)
          And the only thing that could save him
          was the Holy Grail, but see, he forgot
          where he put it. Then it goes ... on
          about — how all the knights in the land
          try to find it — they brought him gold
          and jewels ... but they never worked.
          The King was still dying. Then one day,
          a fool came to the village. And he knelt
          beside the King and sang him some songs.
          Told him some jokes ... But the King
          felt weak and needed a drink. So the
          fool took a cup from beside the bed,
          filled it with water and handed it to
          the King. When the King took the cup, he
          suddenly felt better. And he realized,
          it was the Holy Grail the fool
                  (MORE)

                                          (CONTINUED)

147

> PARRY (CONTINUED)
> had handed to him ... the cup that was
> right beside his bed all along.
> (beat)
> The King said, "How could you find what
> I could not find?" ... and the fool
> said, "I didn't know I couldn't. I only
> knew you were thirsty."

JACK doesn't know how to respond. He's never known PARRY to
be eloquent.

> JACK
> Is that who you are ... my fool?

PARRY turns to face JACK and smiles.

> PARRY
> (suddenly a professor)
> The Fisher King myth has a lot of
> derivations ... I remember I was at this
> lecture in Princeton once. It was this
> awful weekend seminar in Occidental
> Mythology but there was this one
> speaker, Dr. ... uh ... Doctor ... uh
> ... um ...

He stops. As if this memory escaped without any warning.

> ... What was I saying?

JACK is as surprised as he is. PARRY's face is frightened
and confused again. There is panic in his voice.

> ... What was I saying?

JACK grows anxious at PARRY's discomfort, so he covers:

> JACK
> Nothing ... Listen, how come you've
> never asked that girl for a date? ...
> Parry?

But JACK's voice begins to fade away for PARRY. He raises
his head, looks to the outskirts of the field and sees: the
dark silhouette of the RED KNIGHT upon his HORSE. Staring
— knowing exactly where PARRY lies even though it's dark. He
pauses for a moment then gallops off. PARRY watches the RED
KNIGHT ride off. He looks frightened as he lays his head
back down.

JACK'S VOICE comes back and snaps him out of it.

> JACK
> How come you've never asked that girl
> for a date? Parry ...?

(CONTINUED)

148

PARRY snaps out of it somewhat.

> PARRY
> I don't know. I thought it might upset
> our relationship.

> JACK
> Well ... would you go on a date with her
> if it ... happened?

> PARRY
> God yeah.
> (he hears something)
> Sshhh.

They turn on their stomachs and look to the trees.

CUT TO:

Three BLACK YOUTHS; silhouetted by a park lamp, making a
deal beneath a tree.

CUT TO:

A frightened JACK and a suddenly confident PARRY. PARRY
picks up his sling shot, loads a rock, takes aim and fires.

CUT TO:

The rock hitting a nail, whose point secures a rope. The
nail flies off, releasing the rope.

CUT TO:

WIDE ANGLE — THE TREE and surrounding area — as the nets
spring up out of the ground and catapult the YOUTHS up into
the trees.

> BLACK YOUTHS
> HEY! WHAT THE FUCK! SHIT! GET ME THE
> FUCK DOWN FROM HERE!

They continue to complain and curse O.C. as we:

CUT BACK TO:

PARRY and JACK, who suddenly feel safe and more confident.
They lie back down on the grass to continue their
cloudbusting.

CUT TO:

The billowy night clouds slowly drifting apart.

> JACK (O.C.)
> Ha ... Look, they're moving.
> (beat)
> Am I doing that?

JACK HALLUCINATES DURING ROBBERY

This scene had to do with Jack's selfless act. Originally, Jack was to enter Parry's world much more viscerally. He began to have hallucinations, his fear acting as a stimulus. The only hallucinations we kept were the distant sound of hooves (the Red Knight) and the appearance of Edwin shooting his gun. One apparition that was filmed, but did not make it into the final cut, was the appearance of Anne running to Jack's rescue.

We had not seen or mentioned Anne since the end of the second act. I wanted Jack to realize at his most vulnerable moment — when he's dangling from a tower high above Fifth Avenue — that the person he thinks of is Anne. This would lay the groundwork for their reconciliation in the end.

Another hallucination was a moment on the darkened roof, when Jack hears in the darkness a voice that says, "You're being too loud." I liked the eerie effect this created, but it, too was lost in the final shooting.

```
EXT.    CARMICHAEL TOWNHOUSE — MIDDLE OF THE NIGHT

JACK stands on the deserted block in front of the townhouse.
He looks around the neighboring houses — all the New Yorkers
safely locked away behind their doors and windows,
intentionally oblivious to what goes on around them.

JACK is holding a rope with a self-made hook at the end. He
looks up the five story building and takes a gulp. He throws
the rope up. It misses and falls back toward him — scaring
him to jump aside and making an awful sound when it lands.
JACK tries again. It catches. He tugs a bit. He begins to
climb up the front of the townhouse ...

                    JACK
          I was never good at this in gym.

He places a foot on the wall and begins his ascent as he
talks to himself — keeping his terror in check.

                    JACK
               (climbing)
          Listen, I'll just tell them the truth. I
          was stealing a gift for a sick friend.
          Public opinion will be on my side.

He pulls and steps, pulls and steps ... when suddenly — HE
HEARS THE SOUND OF A HORSE GALLOPING TOWARD HIM ...

He stops and slowlly turns to the street, but the street is
vacant — lit by the glow of the street lamp ... An eerie
silence hangs as if for a moment, time stopped.

                                        (CONTINUED)
```

CONTINUED:

                          JACK
          Oh, terrific. I'm hearing horses now.
                    (turns back to the wall)
          Parry will be so pleased! He's finally
          turned me into a moron, too ...
                    (climbing)
          I can just see the headlines. "EX-RADIO
          PERSONALITY TURNS SCREWBALL ON MISSION
          FROM GOD" ... I just hope there's a
          vacant bed —
                    (intensely)
          Right next to his!

JACK hears a siren in the distance and freezes, closing his
eyes:

SUDDENLY, THREE POLICE CARS come barreling down the street —
sirens blasting, they screech to a halt! At least a dozen
COPS hit the streets with rifles and spotlights aimed at
JACK. A REPORTER talks to a news camera on the pavement.

                        REPORTER
          A crazed radio personality dangles from
          the townhouse of billionaire ...

ANNE jumps out of one of the police cars and runs to the
townhouse. Her face is full of concern and love.

                          JACK
                    (seeing her, he whispers)
          Anne.

He is about to call out when we:

                                                  CUT TO:

POV — STREET

IT IS EMPTY AND STILL. A REAL POLICE CAR and siren race down
the adjacent avenue, without any reference to JACK. JACK
blinks his eyes in disbelief — a garbage can stands where
ANNE "stood" ... a page of newspaper blows gently out the top
and across the sidewalk. It was another hallucination.

JACK is a ball of sweat. The fear is peaking. But he gathers
all his strength — takes a deep breath — continues to climb.

AN ALTERNATE ENDING

CAMERA PANS DOWN past the New York skyline the park to reveal JACK and PARRY cloudbusting in the park.

>   JACK
> Beautiful night.

>   PARRY
Mmmmmm.

>   JACK
> You know those Little People you used to hear?

>   PARRY
> Yeah.

>   JACK
> Have you heard from them recently?

>   PARRY
> Sure. Spoke to them last week. They say hi!

They hear muffled voices O.C.

>   JACK
> Ssshhhh.

JACK and PARRY roll over and look toward the trees.

>   CUT TO:

A FOURSOME OF YOUTHS, dealing drugs beneath an elm.

>   CUT TO:

JACK as he calmly picks up THE SLINGSHOT lying by his side on the grass. He stands up, loads, takes aim and fires. WE HEAR the SHOT hitting its target and the "whoosh" of a net being released and swooping the youths up into the trees.

>   YOUTH (O.C.)
>   (in net)
> I'm getting tired of this shit.

JACK picks up a hat with a branch sticking out of it and puts it on his head.

>   JACK
> You think maybe one day I'll get to see them — the Little People?

PARRY looks at JACK — standing naked in the park with a branch sticking out of his head and an excited grin on his face — PARRY smiles proudly.

Interviews with TERRY GILLIAM

by David Morgan

Terry Gilliam has described himself as an optimist who views the world with a healthy degree of skepticism, even though his films have shown the world to be filled with dark, sinister forces. It's a unique sensibility, colored by the art of past eras, and it is proving to be most evident in his evocation of New York City as a magical landscape filled with medieval flourishes and hellish visions of danger.

Born in 1940 in Minneapolis, raised in Los Angeles, and escaped in the '60s to England, Gilliam tested the waters of copywriting and magazine production before stumbling into animation at the BBC and then — with his fellow cohorts in the comic troupe Monty Python — plunging into filmmaking. But despite the quantum leaps in career moves, Gilliam's strong point, what has nourished all his work, has been art and design, which he admits he learned in retrospect. By creating fantastic worlds, and using them as stages for a sense of humor both broad and biting, he has succeeded in capturing on film the very personality which, by nature of his integrity and unashamed contempt for the business side of filmmaking, has been characterized as "visionary." [Or, if you're on the receiving end of his demands, "difficult."]

Hence, the very public fight waged to release *Brazil*, a satire about a terrorized society which some shaken studio executives termed "unreleaseable," yet which surreptitiously won the L.A. Film Critics' top awards in 1985. Or *Time Bandits*, one of the most successful independently-financed films ever made, to the surprise of every major studio which had turned it down.

Irony is something in which Gilliam revels. It is one of the major thematic elements in his work; it's also evident in the fact that Gilliam is again working for a studio — Columbia/Tri-Star — whose former management he feels abandoned his last film, *The Adventures of Baron Munchausen.*

It is *most* telling in the ways the filming and release of his pictures seem to parallel the conflicts and struggles of their storylines, with the director himself living the experiences of his characters. Just as the fight to finish *Munchausen* mimicked the hero's attempts to brave other universes, and the struggle to release "Brazil" in a certain form paralleled Sam Lowry's rebellion against an undaunted bureaucracy, Gilliam again feels a personal stake analogous to the thematic struggle of *The Fisher King* — to regain a clarity of vision after having wandered from the path which one believed would lead to a state of grace.

If such ironic parallels between fiction and filmmaking are indeed repeated here, then the reason why Gilliam is not truly worried about continuing this pattern must lie in the fact that — unlike much of his previous work — *The Fisher King* has a happy, life-affirming ending, so in his mind the completion of this film could only be happy and life-affirming.

It's an idea that can only help keep him going during the first several weeks of production, on location in New York City. An entirely unself-conscious presence on the set, Gilliam is an intense, focused worker, who is nonetheless given to punctuate his speech with facetious jokes and giggles, often at the expense of the difficulties of shooting in the Big Apple. Weather has wreaked havoc upon the filmmakers (it poured three days during the first week, and often enough later on), and the lack of a cover set made it all the more challenging for the director to adhere to the already-tight shooting schedule.

But the logistics have been more or less smooth; a complicated stunt sequence like Parry's mad dash through traffic was completed safely, in one take. Shooting in Grand Central Station went well also, although a problem concerning clearance rights to a song sung by a homeless woman later developed, forcing the filmmakers to return a few weeks later for reshoots. And the effects crew (when they finally do get to go on) have pulled off the Red Knight's shots with aplomb.

The most difficult aspect of shooting in New York has been the size of the place: traffic, noise, crowds of onlookers, all of which prove difficult anyway without the added dangers posed to horse and rider whenever the Red Knight's on call. The main obstacle to the filmmakers, in fact, has been a few bothersome residents who don't appreciate their neighborhoods being filled with smoke.

June, 1990 Interview: During New York location shooting.

Q: When we last spoke near the completion of shooting *Baron Munchausen,* I asked what you had to look forward to; after contemplating suicide, you said you wanted to do something small, perhaps a film with a couple of people in a room and that's it.

And now you seem to have gotten your wish — although you haven't gotten to the room just yet.

Gilliam: The room's always still in the future, yes. I really ran out of steam after *Munchausen.* I think I had reached the point where I was ready to pack in filmmaking, I just was terrified of the whole process.

What happened was, *Watchmen* came along. Joel Silver came along, and convinced me there was this "go" project, and they had a huge budget and all that stuff, and I like *Watchmen* a lot; I think it's really good. And so I got caught up in that thing, and I was actually terrified of it because it was going to be one more monstrous project. But we went along with it; it was weird, because I was sort of propelled forward because it was subject matter I liked a lot, and I knew I could do it, I recognized that I was about the only person who could do it well, and then I didn't get the money. So I was "saved" from that one.

Now, that's what was funny about *Fisher King*: I actually had been sent another script which was the thing I was *supposed* to be interested in. And I read it and I thought it was a bunch of foolishness, and my agent had sent *The Fisher King* along, too.

He said it's a really interesting bit of writing, just look at it. And I did and after the first couple of pages I thought, Jesus , this is terrific. It looked really simple, I understood the characters immediately; with all the attitudes, the characters, I just simply understood [the piece]. Like this medieval element, which is a strange thing because I think it could have been done totally mundane.

And I thought, this is really good; all I've got to do is get a good cast together and *bingo*! it's done, easy. And then, The Demon spoke. He told me "Go Out and Make This!"

Q: You still listen to those Demons.

Gilliam: I keep trying to convince myself that it's not really happening, it's still a little film.

Q: But you've opened up whatever subtext that Richard himself may have been unaware of, but which seems totally truthful.

Gilliam: At some point, I said that I thought that Richard didn't really appreciate or understand the totality of what he had written, of all his themes. But he did on an instinctive, subconscious level. But I sort of pushed it, I've just pushed everything further.

Q: Do you feel more secure in pushing it because it's not your own material? Like you're testing to see how far you can stretch it?

Gilliam: No, actually I feel that I'm trying to be terribly responsible and loyal to the script. I said to Richard, "You know, all I can do now is fuck it up for you." I don't want to do anything [he] wouldn't have wanted. And it's that kind of responsibility that is something I've never experienced. It's really weird; I don't like feeling that I could make a mess of somebody else's idea, and the first couple of weeks I was feeling maybe that's what I was doing. But we're getting on somehow.

Q: How is the film meeting your expectations?

Gilliam: My expectations were really just to have an easy time, and I failed at it. I really just wanted to do something very simple and I find that I can't. No matter how hard I try, to simplify it and do it direct, I elaborate it somewhere, and put the camera in a funny position, make it more of this or more of that.

Q: Yet your elaborations are not taking the story away from what it really is.

Gilliam: I hope not; I mean we'll find that out when I stick it all together. I don't know. This is the stage when I've lost what I set out to do.

Q: Lost?

Gilliam: This is the Parsifal myth; this whole thing is about Parsifal.

Q: You're living the dilemmas of your characters again?

Gilliam: Always, yeah. But the difficulty on this film, is that I'm two characters — I'm Jack *and* Parry. And this is really difficult.

Q: You're the Fisher King *and* the Fool?

Gilliam: Well, they both are; both of them is a Fisher King and both of them is a Fool. But specifically I know both those characters, Parry and Jack, and I'm both of them; normally I'm just one character in the film. In this one I'm both, and it really throws me, and in some scenes I'd started shooting it from a sort of neutral position because I couldn't decide which side I was on. And what's been so good is, Jeff is so grounded in his character, he's pulling me in a direction that is right.

Like the scene we're doing now [in which Parry saves Jack from a pair of thugs] is really from Jack's point of view, and — because I liked what Parry was doing so much — I was featuring Parry more directly. We had set up a whole sequence of shots, and Jeff said, there's a great shot from down here, from between the kid's legs where I was lying, and it suddenly hit me: I've got the wrong point of view on this scene.

Q: Because this was Parry's entrance.

Gilliam: Yeah, I was playing it like Parry coming on, as opposed to Jeff seeing somebody come *into* his life. It depends where you position yourself in it, and

I had put the camera in the wrong place. And so I've adjusted that in my thinking.

Q: Is it progressing in terms of the story that, as Jack becomes totally drawn into Parry's world, effectively becoming Parry, the film gets more and more skewed towards that point of view, where it doesn't show New York for what it is but as Parry himself sees it?

Gilliam: That's what I've been trying from the beginning; the minute Jack steps out of the protective confines of his girlfriend's video store, it goes pretty weird very quickly. It's like in the Parsifal myth: as a boy he sees the Grail, but when he gets to the Grail castle, he doesn't do the right thing. There's a clarity of vision when you're young and then you lose it as you go on, and then you find it at the end hopefully; that's what making the film is like. It was really clear in my mind early on, and now that I'm into it I've lost it, so I'm stumbling through the forest blind at the moment. I'm doing a lot of it by instinct. It's true, that actually is what happens. I'm on auto-pilot right now.

Q: And where are your instincts taking you?

Gilliam: I don't know. We'll find out. I mean, what you do is you make a lot of decisions early on, and set a lot of things in motion, but what happens is then other things start affecting those things you started out with; your original plan is maybe not corrupted but confused by reality. And that's where we are now. I go stumbling on blindly, and everybody says it's terrific, so I trust that it *seems* to be working. I don't actually know what the film is at this point.

Q: Are Jeff and Robin taking you places right now that you didn't expect to go to?

Gilliam: Jeff in particular, because he always does the honest thing. He doesn't do cheap shots. You know, Robin and I have sort of gone for cheap shots to get laughs, to get fun, to get giggles, and Jeff just won't be drawn to those things. He insists on finding his rather strong emotional moments and playing them for real, which is great; it's what the film needs. Because he grounds it all, and then all this madness happens around him, and he is absolutely genuine and I am finding it wonderful. He's making me cry, and basically I'll just sit back and I'll stop my trickery and just settle on Jeff's face and *bingo!*

Q: Is his grounding it allowing Robin to be more wild by contrast? Or does Robin have to pull back to some degree so it won't appear like they're in different movies?

Gilliam: Well, there's a great tension in a way between Robin and Jeff, in the way they play and the way they work, which is what I intended when I first cast the thing. When I first met Robin and we were talking about who would play Jeff, I said it's got to be an actor who doesn't work on the same level as you do; he can't be a funny man, he can't be clever.

Q: Because his character is not like that.

Gilliam: Well, the way it was written, a guy like Eric Bogosian could play the DJ smartass perfectly, but it wouldn't do the job because he disappears; the character's destroyed in the first few minutes of the film and then this *other* character appears who looks the same, and who wears the same clothing, but the guy is different, because he's been so affected by what's happened. And so to get the guy who's the great D.J., we might have ended up with the guy who couldn't do the rest of this film; so I went to the guy who *could* do the rest of the film and then tried to teach him to be a D.J. Which is a bit interesting because you see Jeff's voice is not a D.J.'s voice, but he's been training, and he's turned it into a D.J.'s voice.

Q: There are lots of D.J.s who don't have a "D.J.'s voice."

Gilliam: There's a particular style of D.J., like Howard Stern; it's New York, it's sharp, it's edgy, and it's cynical and sarcastic and that's not Jeff.

Q: But Jeff does seem cynical of Parry, not wanting to follow him, pushing against the idea of Parry and all that Parry claims is real.

Gilliam: Well, that's important because he's dragged into this thing. One of the reasons why I like Jeff doing this is that he can be a real asshole at the start of the thing and you still care about him. You still want to follow him, whereas another actor would be a great asshole and you *wouldn't* care. Jeff is so ... People *like* him, you like him no matter how awful he is. There's something about him that'll drag you along. And I thought that was really important. And that's exactly what he's doing. This is more like "Alice in Wonderland" than anything else [I've ever done]. And Jack is Alice, and he's being dragged into this other world.

Q: And Robin plays every other character.

Gilliam: He starts as the White Rabbit, then he's the Red Queen, he does them all. Parry is such a fractured character; Rob in can be wonderfully pathetic one moment and the next totally silly, and another dangerous and he's all over the place which is wonderful. The more we can make these turns in the character, make him very clear, the better the character becomes I think.

Q: How do you find New York, returning here to work after all these years?

Gilliam: I think it's a much nicer city than it used to be when I was here. Maybe it's me, maybe it's only my perception, but I find it pretty amazing. Going out in the park on a sunny spring day is like some total idyllic existence — the kind of [scene] you used to see at the turn of the century in Berlin or Vienna: people strolling and playing and everybody's out there. That's what it looked like, I couldn't believe it. It seemed like this is a wonderful, wonderful place for everybody. Lately it seems to me the middle classes have been pushed out, so either you're really well off and doing well, and if you're poor it doesn't matter — you're living on the street or you can live in the park. Everybody's out there, it seemed absolutely extraordinary. The homeless thing is uh, I don't think, this isn't about homeless this film. People will want to pretend it is; it isn't. It happens to be the background of the thing, but it's certainly not what it's about.

Q: You've worked before with a couple of members of the crew [most notably cinematographer Roger Pratt, who shot *Brazil*], but most are not experienced to working with you — a situation similar to that of *Munchausen*. How are they (and you) getting used to it? And are you getting back into the drive of being able to shoot and work very quickly?

Gilliam: Not yet. Not the first couple of weeks. It's going rather slowly. The team is coming together. It's a strange situation; to save money they ended up splitting the show between New York and L.A., which ends up that all of the team doesn't play all of the way through the film. I haven't seen what the results of that are going to be yet. And I don't like it because I've never done that before; I mean, you get a team and you go. The key people stay with it, but some of the lesser characters don't, and I'm worried to see about that; I don't know what's going to happen.

Q: You've mentioned before that in your experience, shooting in England, you very much prefer to be a team player, collaborating with everyone in the cast and crew, sharing ideas and ultimately becoming a filter of ideas. And when you were shooting *Munchausen* at Cinecitta Studios in Rome, you described how you as director had been treated by the Italian crew as the maestro, from whom all knowledge and wisdom flows.

Gilliam: The Cult of the "Director-God," yes. I think it's a Catholic thing. You see, if the director can be made God, then people can be popes and cardinals and bishops, and so the greater the director, the greater your popehood is or your bishopric is. And when the Director-God is happy the sun shines, when He's unhappy it rains! So they elevate the director, and consequently if I don't say something, it doesn't happen generally.

It's more of a team in England. That's the nature of the society; people have an attitude that they are more or less equal.

Q: Are you finding that among the crew here, you can be the team player you've been before, as opposed to being thrust into the position of the "Director-God"?

Gilliam: Yeah, I'm very much a team player, but because people don't know me they don't say "No" early enough; they don't say "Wait, hold on a minute, are you *serious* about that?" or "Have you considered maybe there's another way of doing it?" One of the problems here is that they seem to respect me too much. The people I'm working with like the films I've done, and they think I know what I'm doing.

In England people are much better about saying, "Well, why do you want that? Do you really *need* that? Hold on a minute, wait wait wait, let's talk this through."

Q: There are no Devil's Advocates in America?

Gilliam: Not as many as there are in England. I think that's why I was lucky to have ended up in England, because they're less impressed. Here people really are excited about films. And they do love this thing about *"Terry wants something!"* so then everybody runs to make it happen. And they don't always think, "Is that an intelligent thing he was asking for?" And that's the problem of getting older and making more films, too — "The guy *clearly* knows what he's doing; we've seen these films, and are impressed with them." The fact is, he doesn't know as clearly as they *think* he knows what he's doing.

I think I've got to go back and do one in England where people know me better; because people learn as they go along but it's all too late, they've gotten involved with it.

Q: Perhaps it's a good thing that when you go back to California you'll be working with new people!

Gilliam: Maybe! No, it's just, so many people are trying so hard to get themselves nervous on this film. I keep trying to convince myself that it's still a little film. This isn't a difficult film really, but because they've seen *Brazil* and *Munchausen* they want to work on something like that. And when I say "No, we really just need that *little* thing," they don't really believe it.

Q: Are the people on this film trying to make this like *Brazil* and *Munchausen* when it's not?

Gilliam: Well at times it feels like that; I mean, I keep telling people it's … I don't know. I've given up trying to understand *anything*!

What I wanted to do was fight my fantastical side, and I wanted people who were really well-grounded in New York, like Mel Bourne, the designer: he's done Woody Allen films, he knows the nuts and bolts of New York. I spend the whole time trying to ground this film, trying to keep it from turning into a Gilliam film.

Q: And now is it filling up with helium and taking off?

Gilliam: Well, it turned out, everyone wanted to do a Gilliam film except me.

Q: So how do you think their expectations will be met?

Gilliam: I don't know; I think they're getting a Gilliam film!

I keep trying to make it more mundane and drag it down, and everybody says "No, no, you gotta go *this* way." It's very strange. I keep saying, "This isn't *Munchausen*, this isn't *Brazil*." But nobody believes me.

Q: Well, I'm finding similarities: Parry is very much like Baron Munchausen, a character who tries to get others to believe in his version of reality. And the romance, in which the woman in real life comes across as more callous than the fantasy image of her which Parry has, is straight from *Brazil*.

Gilliam: Amanda's great. I think she's probably less callous than the character in the script, because Amanda is just wonderfully mad.

Q: But she has that persona that, no matter what she did, you couldn't help but be drawn towards her, as if she were a little puppy or something. I can see where Parry would pick her out of a crowd even though many people might not even notice her.

Gilliam: That's what was really important to me, to find somebody who could do just that. I was trying to find somebody who didn't look contemporary, with a face that to a modern world is not interesting but to a medieval mind like Parry's would be beautiful. And Amanda is very much like that. To me, I can see exactly why Parry picks her out. She's got this wonderful, long swan neck and a great jawline and, I mean, she's not a contemporary face. I could see her very easily in a tapestry or a medieval painting by Van Eyck. At one point we were trying to give her some long, Rapunzel-like hair so she'd look like a medieval maiden.

Q: You're bringing out a lot of the medieval elements in New York: locations, the design of costumes, the character of the Red Knight, the "castle" serving as the millionaire's townhouse. Are you finding other elements of New York to put in?

Gilliam: Not enough. I mean, they're there but we're not getting them on film. One of the most frustrating parts about this is that all my ideas of gargoyles and bits and pieces — it's all around, it's really easy [to find] in New York, there's *tons* of it — we lose it; we can't go to enough places and shoot enough things quickly.

Q: Can a second unit do that while you're in L.A.?

Gilliam: Uh, I'd want to do it myself. We'll see what happens. I mean the film's not over until it's over. I might be back with a tiny group and get a few goodies.

We shot under the Manhattan Bridge, at the base of that bridge, and it's — well, it's actually not medieval-looking but it's sort of somewhere between Piranesi and Goya. So it certainly doesn't look like New York as we [usually] see it. At an entrance to the side of the bridge there's a great arch, which we use as Jack's passage into Parry's underworld. "Abandon all hope ye who enter here" is what it should have over it.

At times the thing is like "Alice in Wonderland" and Dante and Virgil, it's all these things. There's a statue of Dante right outside my hotel. I can see him when I look out my window, in a little square right opposite Lincoln Center — there stands Dante.

Q: Is that an omen of some kind?

Gilliam: Of course. We were getting very worried that some of the stuff that we were doing is a bit zany. And we keep trying to insert ugliness in it, and a certain brutality, because it could be "Home Free" — it could be that show. Parry's a really good bum, but we're trying to make it so that when Parry does have his hallucinations they're really ugly; he's disturbing.

Q: And dangerous to other people.

Gilliam: Yeah. I just hope I'm getting it on film. But again, that's where Jeff is so good because even when Parry's crazy, Jeff is angry at him and at his reaction to him. And they've both done really touching moments too, where they sort of come together.

I think what will make the film, what's going to be interesting, is whether all the elements which each in its own right is very rich and good, whether they all fit together and they don't compete; that'll be the fun of it. Editing at the end, just balancing all these things so that everything — the sort of spectacular way that I'm shooting it and these strange angles and all that — don't affect the performances and the characters because that's what it's about: the characters. I'm just trying to put them in a world that is more spectacular than most.

Q: Looking at the dailies, can you tell? For example, the footage of the Red Knight galloping down Fifth Avenue: does it look like it might be out of place or work against the rest of the film?

Gilliam: As I said I don't know. I really don't; I'm on auto-pilot now. I don't have a fucking clue; I just shoot the stuff! I'm sure you won't tell *anybody* this, because they don't want to believe that, but it's *true*! I mean, even the actors; we all are working on this premise — you plan and you talk about it and you rehearse and then you have to start working by instinct and just *doing* it.

And I've been worrying more on this film than I have on anything else because it's not mine, and I feel this greater responsibility; with my own scripts I can say, "Oh fuck it, I don't care." I'll just do it. And this, I can't do that. I mean, we all worry it to death; Robin worries to death, Jeff worries, we all worry all the time.

Q: Does Richard worry as well? Or is he in seventh heaven, thinking, "Hey, Robin Williams and Jeff Bridges and Terry Gilliam are making *my* movie!"

Gilliam: It started that way but then the reality comes in, when we start fucking around with it, and he's been getting better at fighting back when it really starts becoming violated in any way. I always refer to him, always, to make sure that we aren't violating his sensitivity towards it, because it's his idea. So whatever I do, I always double check with him. Because if he feels comfortable with it then on we go. If he doesn't, we talk about that. I think it's the only way I can work on this film. He is around the whole time, which is great because I want him there.

Robin always changes the lines, and Richard said he couldn't believe that he's *enjoying* that process, that his words aren't sacrosanct, even though they were all his. Robin sort of stumbles on other things that are better sometimes, sometimes not, but I don't see the point in restricting Robin, because that's what he's about: these things that pop out. Some work and some don't. You don't want to lose that. That and also, it makes it harder for him if he can't enjoy what he's doing; when he's enjoying something he's throwing ten million ideas out and I get a good performance out of him. He's got to feel comfortable, so we do it, we try this, we try that.

While Robin is like a scattergun approach, a shotgun, Jeff is just very, very precise.

Q: Like a rifleshot.

Gilliam: Yeah. Robin does this flurry of punches — some hit, some don't — Jeff just waits and does the left jab, *bing*! Short shot but it works every time, never misses. It's great to see the two things working like that.

Q: Are you buffered from the studio by the producers?

Gilliam: Yeah, they seem to be very supportive. I can't complain at all. I wish I *could*. But I can't. The important thing is that what they're seeing has impressed them and they like it, and that's the proof really. I mean, they were very nice at the beginning; I think they were very wary because of the *Munchausen* debacle.

Q: What *did* you learn from that?

Gilliam: What, *Munchausen*? Not to make *Baron Munchausen* again. I learned not to work with a particular producer again.

No specific things, there's no grand wisdom that's acquired by that. You've just got to be more careful. But on the other hand, if we had been more careful we wouldn't even have started the process, and there's a film there at the end of it, which is important.

So you can't really say [the experience] was bad because if we had been more reasonable and careful and intelligent we wouldn't have gotten the thing off the ground.

There's a certain madness, a combination of people that at least started the ball rolling; once it started rolling you couldn't stop it. It rolled over a lot of people including me, but a film came out at the end, that's all I know, which is important.

[On this picture] we've had certain problems in the first couple of weeks, it's just been really rough here; New York is impossible to work here, and we've, uh, slipped a bit. I began to think, "Oh it's *Munchausen* all over again."

Q: But you also have a much tighter budget this time [$23 million, split evenly above and below the line], whereas *Munchausen* started off with a blank check.

Gilliam: No, it didn't. Starting off it was very carefully budgeted except totally unrealistically. The figures didn't match the reality of what we were doing.

Q: Is this budget realistic even though it is tight?

Gilliam: It *better* be. I don't know. I am slightly at a disadvantage having never [filmed] here, I don't know what the money buys, but we've gone through it and it seems to be right. To be fair they, meaning Debra Hill and Lynda Obst, have not produced a film as ambitious as mine normally are. And I think it's hard for people; they don't seem to understand what it means when I say "I want something like *this*." Even I don't; that's one of the reasons I ask for it. But a certain naïveté makes you think you can do it and if you *think* you can do it, you have a go.

The last couple of days were very silly where we're doing a close-up of Jeff in front of Carmichael's townhouse, against those stairs which were built in California, with all of Madison Avenue behind us, with buses. The noise is unbearable, it's ruining sound takes, and I'm shooting stuff like that. And I used to laugh at people who did things like that, it's ridiculous; you could do that close-up in L.A. — just bring the stairs back. But we end up doing it because everybody's fired up, you've got to do it. Yesterday we did close-ups with the Knight on Fifth Avenue, and what you see on film, I'm not sure if you know it's Fifth Avenue, which is very, very bad. But it's to do with the fact that you get away with it, is why you do it.

[The Manhattan Bridge location] again is a silly thing. We just stood here and said, "Oh wouldn't that look nice as a background?" Well, what is involved in *making* it a background is crazy, and for somebody to have said "You can't do that" would have saved us a lot of trouble; you could have done this scene just on a corner somewhere, but nobody said no, so here we are.

This little idea came up, I was watching rush hour traffic in Grand Central. There's a scene that took place at rush hour, and I thought, "Wouldn't it be great if all these people suddenly started waltzing?"

Q: And people took you seriously.

Gilliam: [shrugs] Nobody said no!

Q: Are you expecting that one day somebody *will* come in and say "No"? Because on *Munchausen*, nobody told you "No" until it was too late to do anything about it.

Gilliam: Way out of control, yeah. The problem is the ideas seem to capture people, and everybody — not just me but everybody else — falls victim to these things. It's weird; ideas do this.

Then you discover, it isn't just the waltzing; the pictures have got to look right. Then I want the lights in a certain way. It's all the details. That is the difference in shooting it with bad lighting and shooting it with good lighting; good lighting costs more money. What's interesting, when you work with good people, it doesn't really come out cheaper because their demands are greater. Really good people are full of ideas and they work to a higher standard. And you pay for it; it costs money. It doesn't come really cheap.

Q: How is your working relationship with the department heads you've not worked with before?

Gilliam: The interesting thing with films is that the pattern is very quickly established. And because everybody knows that I'm involved in the design of everything on my films, when they walk in they know they're going to be involved with me. I stick my nose in much more than a lot of other directors might.

Q: So you're not frightening them away.

Gilliam: No, I don't think so. Good people, at least most of the ones I can think of, really like input. My problem is that I just have pretty clear ideas about a lot of things. And until I sort of get them I don't let up. But there's no way that I can credit myself for all this stuff.

Like with the costumes for Jeff's character: I wanted Versace clothes because I wanted the most expensive, sleekest stuff at the beginning. Jack's a guy who's really a product of America's materialism, all style and fashion — the best, slick, cool. But everything is monochromatic with him; there's blacks and greys, no color. And I like the idea of trashing his Versace clothes when he becomes a bum, which is really silly when you're paying two thousand dollars for a suit and you're trashing it.

Q: Jack's lost his job, he's lost his home, but he doesn't want to give up his clothes so he wears them into the ground .

Gilliam: Uh-hmm. I also like the idea of seeing these very expensive clothes look like shit.

It's been slightly harder on costumes for me because they're contemporary things and I don't have any great feeling [for them], and so [costume designer] Beatrix Pasztor and I would just spend a lot of time together, and Jeff is very full of ideas. Everyone's got ideas, that's what's nice about it, and I just become the guy who sort of guides it through and says "I like that" and "I *don't* like that."

Basically Jeff's costumes are the result of Jeff, Beatrix and I sitting in a room for hours on end, trying things on, all shifting around.

Robin, the same thing: Parry had to have this medieval aspect, and what's nice is that it's all real modern stuff. With that cape and that poncho and hat, he really comes out of a Bruegel painting. And underneath it he's got this bit of gold lamé, looks like some golden fleece or a bit of chain mail. And all that's been good fun, to try and assemble what is believable and yet has this total medieval quality to it.

It's nice working like that. You know, I think a lot of directors just don't do any of that stuff. They just hire the costume people, the costume people say, "Bum bum bum, this is how we're gonna do it," the financing's all right and that's the end of it. I just think that takes the fun out of it.

It's always like doing a painting. You just want to have all the parts the way you'd like them in a painting. I mean, on this one, I'm paying much less attention to background than I normally do because it doesn't seem to be what this film is about.

Q: This isn't a case where there's always something going on very deep in the frame?

Gilliam: No, I'm not doing that on this one, I'm just tired of looking back there any more. I don't want to lose the characters in that sort of deep photography; I want to keep them in the center. I hope I pull it off.

Q: Well, the thing you can most easily get away with is the vision of the Red Knight, because people would *expect* it to be fantastical.

Gilliam: I don't know if the Red Knight is going to be the weirdest thing in this film; I'm beginning to think maybe the rest of it is as fantastical as the Red Knight. I'm having this feeling that the Red Knight is going to be soundless. Because everything else in New York is so noisy, the thing to make it frightening is if there's no sound to it.

Q: Seen but not heard.

Gilliam: Yeah, like children should be.

March, 1991 Interview: During final editing of the picture.

Q: One of the most striking things about the film is the dichotomy between Jack's world and Parry's. In all the scenes in which Jack is in his disk jockey world, New York looks extremely oppressive — very sleek, cold, monochromatic, and he seems trapped by it. And it's only when he can get out and breathe the air on the Lower East Side when he's with Parry that he can actually become a human being and associate with others on a more human level.

Gilliam: Yeah, I think that's pretty consistent through all my stuff. I think it all basically springs from the fact that I lived in New York after college for three years; most of the attitudes I put in my films are based on that period. And I find it's a strange place, New York — I mean, all cities are strange, but New York in particular because I think it's more of an extreme version of what a city can be. And I'm always torn by them because on one hand they're this center of incredible activity and energy and massed humanity and I get a real buzz off of that; but then at the same time it seems to crush people. It reduces people to cogs in the machine or molecules within a system, whatever, and that part just drives me crazy, when individuals get lost to be aspects of the machinery.

I remember my first view of New York was getting out of the subway at 42nd Street, coming from the airport, and that was just *Whough!* There you are at the bottom of these monoliths and it's exhilarating and terrifying at the same time, and so I try to deal with that.

Q: Do you see New York differently now than when you first lived and worked there?

Gilliam: I actually thought New York had gotten to be quite a jolly place. I mean I don't know if that's a product of having money now, rather than being poor in New York, where I can actually stay in nice hotels, go to nice restaurants and see the good sides of the city. That may have a lot to do with it, because when I lived there, I had no money at all; it's like you feel you're at the bottom of all those great towers the whole time, and everybody else is up there having a good time except you. The streets were where you were left. I didn't actually like the streets because I in my heart of hearts wanted to be up in the top of the towers. The streets, I mean they were lively but when you're trying to get away from them they're not as interesting as when you've just submitted to them and allowed them to take over. I mean it's that kind of a thing: when you aspire to those towers, when you get up there, it's the world that Jack's inhabiting on many occasions; you've lost yourself in the process.

Q: So you have to clamor back down to the streets.

Gilliam: Yeah, that's where I feel happier now. At least there are people down there, because it's all about humanity. And the higher you get the more isolated you get, the more separate from humanity you become. And again you get lost in yourself, you become isolated within yourself. And that's a part of what this film is certainly about.

Jack's world is all about design and it is very photogenic, everything is minimalist. It's reduced to the bare bones, and yet everything he's in is a cage of one sort or another, or a glass tank. He's isolated from the world totally, by all these man-made things. We've got his radio studio, there's no windows — that's one box he's in. We actually put all those little shadows around to make it look like a cage almost. And he's on his own, he's not even in direct communication with his crew, who are on the other side of this glass barrier. And his only contact with the world is through machines, the telephone — it's nothing that's direct.

Everything is distanced and made safe in a sense that he doesn't have to get dirty, he doesn't have to rub shoulders with anybody. He's in his limo or his agent's limo and the world is knocking at his window and he won't open the window.

Q: And it's one-way glass; the world can't even see him.

Gilliam: Yeah, that's right. And then his apartment we made a bit cage-like. It was like, is this where the modern, sleek, stylized world is going? Everything he's got is the best the modern material world offers, but there's a tendency for it to lead to isolation and really losing touch with anything natural or God-made as opposed to man-made. And there he is; it's a barren environment he lives in, and he's a prisoner of it. There's nothing alive in there. Everything is very anal, it's all controlled. He's controlled his life he thinks, but by controlling it he's allowed nothing to get into it. And it becomes a very empty life.

He's a prisoner of his desire for success. It's the kind of success that I'm afraid love of the modern world aspires to, and in a sense encourages. So that's what all that was: pretty obvious stuff!

Q: Now when you were shooting exteriors, New York was speaking to you in a certain way.

Gilliam: Yeah, it was *shouting* at me, and it wouldn't shut up!

Q: What sort of influence did Los Angeles have on you when you suddenly went onto a soundstage, secluded on a little set, to shoot the interior scenes?

Gilliam: That was one of my big fears, and that's why people like Mel Bourne were to me very important. All of us were worried that we would slide back into the soft, somnambulant world of L.A. where everything's easy and smooth, because in New York you're actually working against this barrage of noise wherever you are. Inside or outside, there's noise. You just feel the energy of the city all around you all the time, at least I do. It's really an annoyance but it's there. And it makes you talk, move, do everything a bit faster, louder, quicker, whatever.

We spent a lot of time just pushing extras and everybody to make them move faster. There's this shot, it's not actually in the film now, where Jack followed Lydia into her office building and he rides the elevator up and follows her out, and it was just the extras, trying to get them out of the elevator — they were all incredibly *polite*!

Q: They were not true New Yorkers.

Gilliam: Yeah, whereas in New York, they'd push and shove you to get on; "Come on, get out of the way! Everybody's late!"

It was a constant effort all the time to maintain that kind of energy, and I think basically we've done it. I mean luckily, some of the big scenes here were just dependent on Robin, or Jeff and Mercedes. In fact all of the interiors except for the Chinese restaurant were done in L.A. And I watch it, and I'm really pleased, I think we got it. And again what helps is working on the soundtrack — adding police sirens, crowds ...

Q: Adding even *more* noise.

Gilliam: You should never stop, really. I mean New York, I used to sleep with ear plugs on, because I couldn't sleep with the noise.

Q: And yet the Red Knight makes no noise at all.

Gilliam: Ah, he does a little bit now. There's whispers in the air. It's as quiet as you can get. Actually I got a choir to whisper and it works very well because it's sort of like all the voices in Parry's head somehow, but they're not screaming and shouting; they're going *buzz-buzz-buzz* which is much more insidious and disturbing.

Q: At this stage what are some of the responses you've had to the film?

Gilliam: I find it quite funny when you come out to L.A.; it's a City of Fear. Not L.A., it's the Hollywood aspect of L.A. They live in such fear and they go to these screenings and they have all these cards they give the audience, trying to find out what the public are like: "Who *are* these people out there?" It's like they've lost their gut instincts; they've disassociated themselves from humanity by the world they've created. It's a strange one.

I find when I get out of L.A. and start showing the film, you start getting responses that I trust much more, because there's less vested interests. There aren't enough brave people out here; I think you just go to the film, you just go, and if you operate out of confidence, I think you'll make better choices.

Q: How long is it right now?

Gilliam: Just right. It's about I think 2:17, 2:18, that's with the credits, but the kind of cuts that are being discussed literally are about four minutes, which doesn't get it down to the magic two hours.

We had a good screening on Friday night. We're doing another one tonight, just to let the studio try a few changes that they have in mind, to convince me that they're right and I'm wrong.

Q: Will they be able to?

Gilliam: I doubt it. I mean, unless somehow there's this massive leap in the cards, which I somehow don't think will happen.

The cards no matter what we do with the film just about stay the same. And the problem is, because the cards are so good, they think that by shortening it a bit they'll get even *better*.

Q: I did see the first rough cut; how does this present version differ from that, apart from the music score and final sound mixing?

Gilliam: It's about four minutes shorter. Actually it's amazing — four minutes if they're in the right place make all the difference in the world. I find some of the things that are being asked now are just very crude and I don't think that they really work. But anyway we'll see.

That's always my problem: being both open and sensitive to what people think and how they react to things, and at the same time keep listening to whatever inner voice is telling me to do this, that or the other thing. And I never quite work out that balance because that's the nature of the game, just trying to tread that tightrope.

Interview with ROBIN WILLIAMS

by David Morgan

During the several weeks of location shooting in New York, Robin Williams can usually be found in between takes entertaining the actors, P.A.'s and grips by riffing on some bit of business: a silly sound effect or wry non sequitur, or more serious commentary on the air of censorship surrounding current art exhibitions, television programs and books. [One entertaining routine of his melts together *Poltergeist* and *Cool Hand Luke*, as he impersonates Strother Martin declaring "What we have here is a failure to excommunicate!"]. He definitely helps make the long stretches of time waiting for camera setups passable.

Yet he may just as often be found standing off on his own, quiet, deep in thought, away from unnecessary sensory overload. Crew members avoid or ignore him at these private moments; he therefore seems not unlike the anonymous, withdrawn homeless people on the fringes of the production. Williams is also less recognizable at these moments, less likely to elicit shouts of "Ro-bin!" or "Hey, Mork!" from passing bicycle messengers.

One surprising aspect of Williams' personality which comes across in conversation is the vulnerability he feels while shaping a difficult performance. He clearly respects Gilliam's vision and direction, and seems to acquiesce to whatever judgments Gilliam makes, such as the success of each day's rushes (which Williams avoids attending). Perhaps acting on equal footing with a "real" actor as opposed to a fellow comedian has also left him feeling more challenged, and less sure of his limits. Consciously or unconsciously, he appears to be trying very hard to please everyone (not just himself) with his performance, even when Parry threatens to overshadow his surroundings.

When stopping to discuss the complexities of the role, Williams at first seems closed in. Dressed in an oversized Versace suit for a scene in which he runs up Amsterdam Avenue in a manic fit, Williams sits constricted, his arms wrapped around his crossed legs, only over time gradually stretching out, loosening up. He speaks quietly and thoughtfully, carefully examining his own reactions to the emotional pull of the story and only occasionally punctuating the discussion with jokes, making one suspect that he takes his work much more seriously than he does himself.

• • •

Q: Although you had worked with Terry on *Munchausen*, this is the first time that one of Terry's films has featured stars who stood above the environments he created for them.

Williams: Normally they're just small cameos, people coming and going. Like *Time Bandits*: Sean Connery was even a cameo.

Q: Although they were entertaining that wasn't necessarily what held the film together. Here it really is the performances that are the core of the film, regardless of how spectacular the visuals may be. So how is it different working with Terry now?

Williams: I don't think people thought that he directs in the way that he's doing this — really toning things down to where characters are talking, trying to simplify this. I think they all assume that with him it's just visuals. He *talks* to people; he has to. I kid him about it; I tell him it's just a four-character Gilliam film with a big knight. But he's got to [simplify], because the stuff lives on that.

I was even surprised by the *way* Terry talks. The first time I saw it was in Grand Central Station, where he had that homeless character singing a song, and she was very frightened and he went in just to talk to her, then all of a sudden she kicked out. He just said, "Let it go, forget all these things, these people watching you, and just do it." And she just blew the place off, because he let her be what she is, this wonderful gospel singer. He said just put it in, and she did it. She got applause even from people on the side: "Yeah, I like that, that woman's good!"

I just saw something wonderful happen. There's *something* happening here, and people in the crew see that. One night there was a great thing, and Richard was sitting there, and a guy, a grip or somebody who was just listening to it, said, "Who wrote this? Did *you* write this? Wow, it's really nice." He was kind of blown away by it. It's like, I knew *Dead Poets* worked when I saw a Teamster cry over it. Okay, there's something good there; it got to him.

I don't go to dailies but from what Terry says, the simplest stuff seems to just shine through. It's kind of heartening, keeps everything going. Even last night shooting at the Chinese restaurant, he said it was interesting to see four separate marks; Jeff and Mercedes are doing something kind of wonderful and sexy in the back, and Amanda and I are doing something in the front, like two little kids playing and romping.

You know why Terry took this — he liked it, and it was a test for him to try this, to deal with the humanity of it, along with the imagery which he's incredible at. It's interesting to me to talk to him about that, and it's usually very simple stuff he talks about.

Q: You say you haven't been going to dailies?

Williams: I ask about them, just to keep a work-in-progress thing of what's up. Some day we'll have to go.

Q: But you can't?

Williams: No, I can't see myself.

Q: Just because it's this early on?

Williams: I can't do it, ever. Because if I do I'll be fixating on the wrong things. Or later, playing the game of, when the film comes out saying, "Well, I saw something better."

Q: "Why didn't he use that other take?"

Williams: Yeah, and it's *his* choice. So it's like, okay.

Q: But you do examine the playback monitors in between takes. What do you look for?

Williams: Sometimes I do, to see how it's framed. If it's a movement, how can I block it out, or am I gonna get run over by the horse? Can I be closer to the horse, or farther away?

Q: Or if you try out some physical gag, like in front of Carmichael's when you're talking to passersby and they don't even want to look at you, to see how it plays?

Williams: Yeah, like when I'm dancing around. And then you see and you say "Oh, great." Then sometimes you have to worry "Oh, shit, my hat fell off!" Can I do something to cover it, because that looked wonderful. Especially wide shots where things are going nuts, can I do *more*? Usually I ask, "Can I try something else?" Then you see it and say no, you don't need any more.

Q: But you also have to be conscious of the way a scene's being framed, the angles, the lenses used. That must affect how you decide to act out a scene.

Williams: Yeah, this isn't being shot like normal. It's a lot of angles that are ups and downs and sides and overs. One of the initial premises he said was, no one in New York looks up. It *is* like that. Very few people are looking up all the time, but you've got all these incredible things around you: architecture, gargoyles, a lot of medieval shit.

Q: When you were just running up Amsterdam going crazy, you stopped at the corner, turned and saw the Knight. He then shot that closeup of you a couple of ways, with different lenses, putting you on top of a box right underneath the traffic signal, to distort the background even further.

Williams: That's very strange stuff. You want to know, well is that *too* much? It's weird too, 'cause in the end something may look wonderful on the monitor, and then you see it on the screen it just looks grotesque, it's just *way* over. He said that about some of the stuff at Carmichael's. We were lucky, we had some time, we did some other closeups and just took it back down again. Be cause it was once again playing mad versus just *being* mad — stopping and just focusing on Jeff, just talking to him and not having to put all that on. Because it's bizarre enough the way I look, that you don't have to add a lot.

I check the monitors, but it's weird because, number one, they're not in color, and number two, they're small. Terry said when you see it on the big screen, all of a sudden things he never saw on the monitor show up: wonderful little movements, tiny things that read huge or read big!

Q: What sort of guidance does he give you for your character? In *Munchausen* you played an off-the-wall character in an off-the-wall place; here you're sometimes an off-the-wall character in a place that to the rest of us is at least fairly normal.

Williams: There are times when he deals with that world very realistically. Then it's the old thing: how do you *play* madness ? It's what they see at that given moment. The most interesting thing we found out was, first of all you don't have to yell; even though it was outside, the camera is picking up everything. Second of all, it was switching — going from one moment being wild and going to the next moment being very calm, and then the next moment being like *that* again.

It's like the people you see around here. Two nights ago there was a guy who was pretty wigged out, watching us with the Red Knight. And you could see for him it was like a documentary. He was going "Yeah, I like that. You *did* it." For him it wasn't any great hallucination; it was like, "Yeah, I've seen that, too!"

Q: Like it was his reality already.

Williams: Yeah, he thought we were kind of making it for him. It's a real mixed bag here: you've got kind of up-tempo people and real burned-out people coming through. It's a real interesting thing. And it kind of highlights what we're talking about; you see it when you see the real thing walk by. A guy flipped out the other night, he just started screaming and then he got very calm, then he started talking about peace and love, and then he'd blurt out "But I'll *kill* ya!" And that's what Terry was really talking about, how to make the dichotomy work.

It's changing gears and being in each one separately, to be full out and then go back to this kind of stillness. He said the piece could bear it. He's kind of shocked by it; I think he envisioned it going one way and now it's going full-out crazy and then it comes back to these very quiet moments, and then back out into madness.

And then he said, when in doubt we can go simple, because we know what "out there" is and we can always try "out there" and just focus on that. Like out in the park, the Fisher King story. We worked it out, took about five different pieces and kind of blended them together, kind of made an Amish quilt of all these different drafts and put them together and told the story. And he says he'll probably stay with no cuts, which is kind of frightening. I thought "You sure you're not going to need to go away?" He said no.

It's weird. Between Terry and Jeff, I learn a lot. When I go with Jeff I'm real comfortable with him. Jeff is very methodical about things, but also he has an incredible way about how he is in the shot. For me usually I throw everything out there and ask "Well, what do you want to try *now*?" My world is kind of skewed, at least the way he shoots it, especially when it gets crazy, and then there are other times when it's beatific. And sometimes it's like Dante, other times it's like Groucho, and it goes back and forth. But still, trying to keep that straight line, and plus the human connection among the four of us … it's *weird*.

And the last two nights it's just been me wigging out, running down the street, just going full out. It was great today. Here's another example of some specific directions: what Terry'll do sometimes is just tell me what the image is he's going to put with this shot, so it's not much direction, it's just telling you what you'll be put against or with, and work from that. He describes some pretty horrifying and amazing images that go back-to-back: my wife getting shot, the next image is of dancing and her hair will be flowing, and then these are some things I'll work on when I run, so it just doesn't become general ranting and raving.

Q: On the page it seems incredible, all the memories flowing back over your character.

Williams: It's a full breakdown. Finally at the very end, after screaming and groveling before he gets beaten up, he's just devoid, he's snapped, he's catatonic. When the punk stabs him, I don't think he even feels it.

So it's weird. I'm exhausted. I felt when I started, "Yeah, I'll just be riffing around," but *nooooo*.

Q: It must take a lot just to keep that level of energy.

Williams: Yeah. Last night I got just about seven. It was weird; we were inside that Chinese restaurant shooting the dinner scene and outside it's a beautiful day. It's like "There's something very strange about this. Doctor Leary? Pick up the red phone!"

I think it's interesting for Terry because he has to deal with these elements and not miniatures or huge sets, even though he is doing that at times. I mean, the shot under the Manhattan Bridge is equal to anything in *Munchausen*. People will see, just the way he's shooting New York, some is so romantic, and some is so grotesque.

Q: But he's been very conscious of not putting as much stuff in the background of the scenes in this film.

Williams: Well, he had little people in Grand Central Station. I think he started off doing that, and then he realized he had to pull back from it.

Q: Or only use it in very selectively.

Williams: Uh hmm. Keep it kind of strange but then pull back.

Q: Eric Idle had suggested once that he thought Terry got great performances in his films almost by default because his attention seemed so taken with the visuals — he'd just let the actors do their thing and not worry about them. I think that's an exaggeration, but in *Fisher King* he seems to be paying more attention to them as a director, and also not filling the frame with a lot of peripheral characters or business which might be distracting.

Williams: The meticulous thing he did was to pick the right combination of people. It isn't random, he didn't just pick people, "Well, we'll get these, they'll do." Like Amanda, at one moment she could be wonderfully awkward and the next moment be gorgeous. He said on film she's stunning. All of a sudden she does look like something out of the Renaissance. He said when he saw the screen test it was perfect, that one moment she could be very beyond plain, make white bread seem spicy, and then the next moment be exquisite. And Jeff, he met with him and talked with him and I think even Jeff wasn't sure, and then we were working through it and we realized it *was* the perfect choice, because he really is great. Terry picked him for a reason; here I am wigging out, this mad abandon, and then there's this man who's like an anchor.

Q: Terry says that he feels Jeff is grounding him; sometimes he'd envision a scene and follow all the action and craziness that you might be playing, and then discover that it should be seen through Jeff's eyes, and so he'd pull back to the emotional center that Jeff was representing.

Williams: I think that's what he does.

Q: Do you find you're grounding *yourself* more because of Jeff, or is his anchor allowing you to be even wilder, more experimental?

Williams: Well, no, two things; it lets me go crazy because number one, I know he's there, and also when it's time to come back again —

Q: There's somebody there waiting for you.

Williams: Yeah, and he can get real, real simple with it. Real. And I have to worry about it. And they say at the times when it happens there's this amazing kind of interplay, that it seems to work, back and forth. I'm someone just doing all these bizarre things but still coming back and connecting to Jeff, being very rational for a few brief minutes and then going off again. So I sort of suck Jeff through it, take him into this world, and in the end bring him out. Yeah, he grounds me a lot. Grounding isn't the word because it makes it seem like *"Oh, you're grounded!"*

He frees the shit out of me, too, in many ways, because I'm not afraid to try stuff; and then the greatest thing is that I'm not afraid to do *nothing*, to just stop for a moment, and in that I find this incredible power. For instance, when he tries to offer me money and I don't know what to say, I just look at him, it's quite powerful and very strange — not pathetic but very moving, in a sense that you end up not knowing what to say. Someone is willing to give this money, the first human gesture he's seen in a long while.

I don't think anybody expected the film to be changing the way it does, how the things are turning out. I knew this stuff was good, there were bits that were very surreal, but I think it's getting a depth to it, and a pain in some ways that I never saw. Even the vision of the Red Knight: when you get into it, you realize it's deeply painful stuff. Sometimes horrifying, sometimes moving. I never envisioned it that way.

Q: Shooting in New York must add to the surrealism.

Williams: Yeah! You know, if anyone ever says, "How can these characters dress like this?" Come here, look; look at the guy over there dressed like a ninja in Hefty bags. And the balls we used in the opening sequence, that was taken from a guy down at Tompkins Square Park, and whether it was a weapon or something he felt was attractive, I don't know. It's all here.

Shooting at night here is like some sort of Truffaut film, because you've got everything going on, and then there's the real thing there watching you. They're cheering you on, or sometimes flipping out, or sometimes participating. It's very strange. I'm glad they let us shoot as much as they did here in New York.

Q: Are you finding it a distraction though, with all the noise and crowds?

Williams: It is. There's a lot of wonderful stuff, because of the look, the feel, the reality of it; yet as interesting as it is, there's a lot of negative stuff: the noise, the people who do get angry, the people who call up the fire engines, "What is it , macaroni on fire?" Shit!

Q: One woman tried to hurl a bucket of water at the Red Knight from her apartment window!

Williams: Yeah, they saw fire, they wanted to get the film crew out. You know, it's their life, this is their neighborhood. When you're shooting on their street it's exciting for about an hour and then they realize, these people are going to be here for three days. "Screw this!" But on the whole most people are great with it.

Q: So what is this role providing you which you haven't been able to explore previously?

Williams: This is probably more than anything else just a full gamut of everything: it's got a nervous breakdown from *Seize the Day*; it has full manic things that are almost like stand-up; it has elements of *Dead Poets* in terms of the classic nature of some events, only a sprinkling though. It's like a "Greatest Hits," combined with this greatly pained man who has this wonderfully skewed view of the world caused by an incredibly traumatic event. That's what's interesting for me. I didn't realize how hard it was going to be when I started. I thought, Oh Lord, so easy! After about a day I went *Oops*! Guess I better bring out all that research stuff now. Because you have to know exactly how and what, even in those things like you said when you're seeing the Knight, not just knowing what it is but what's *underneath*. You keep that thought kind of boiling underneath, and ask Terry, "Can I do that take again?"
  Because it isn't just terror, it isn't just some knight. It's what we found when I did the first reactions upon seeing the knight: it's a heavy duty psychological and physiological reaction. Quite grotesque, quite horrifying. So after that day I walked back like, *yeah, this is fun*! Sure, this is a little light character comedy!
  That's what's been interesting. This is really a balanced piece, and balanced in the writing, too. It's like some great piece of music, because the musicians all have great things to do. It balances out, and also we pick very strong people; each one of them is just as strong as the others. It's knowing when to back up. Like the thing with Amanda the other night [as they stumble through a Chinese

meal], knowing that that'll be a wonderful part for her and then I'll come in with some shtick, and then she finishes.

Q: But what's intriguing, and at times frustrating, is that we have gotten to know two characters, Parry and Jack — and Parry and Lydia as well — who each inhabit their own particular worlds, and we get to see them gradually fall into sync with one another while doing these goofy things, or fighting their instincts which tell them to go the other way. It would be very easy for that kind of interplay to turn silly, or unreal.

Williams: Yeah. It's very delicate. It's like the glass animals in *Glass Menagerie.* I've tried a few things and it just was like *whoops!* Sorry, leg snapped on the deer, there it goes. It's that delicate, and that's what's interesting — and it's hard. And then there's full-out madness and violence. Under the bridge, Terry said it was this wonderful thing; it looks kind of funny but then it's really very painful and very violent, when the black drunk grabs Jeff and shoves the shit in his face. It's like, these aren't quaint people. These aren't the guys you're going to hang around with and have great conversation: "Yeah, *fuck* you boy! *Fuck* it!"

Yeah, that's why I find you can go so many places; it'll be interesting to see how the pieces work. I don't think this would be like any other movie. I mean, it has elements of different things, but it has its own weight, its own momentum. I'm really curious to see how it all fits. So is Terry.

Q: And it is a very delicate balancing act.

Williams: It is. It's all about how much will the weight bear — how surreal? How violent? Well, you keep walking that line.

Q: Is there anything you're particularly anxious about?

Williams: To see the Grand Central Station scene. I just want to know what that's like. Following her, the whole world spinning with this beautiful music, and then she disappears. If it works it will be incredible; if it doesn't work, it's a very interesting travelogue, a nice brochure for Grand Central Station.

Q: That wasn't in the script originally; what was your reaction when it was suggested?

Williams: When they described it I went, "That sounds amazing. Are they really going to *pay* for that?"

David Morgan is a New York-based journalist, editor and screenwriter who covered the production of *The Adventures of Baron Munchausen* for *Sight & Sound*. He has contributed film reporting and analysis to the *Los Angeles Times*, *Millimeter* and *Metropolis* [in which excerpts from the above interviews originally appeared], as well as to *Blitz*, *Cinefex* and *Movieline*.

Symposium

MEL BOURNE,

I thought, before meeting Terry, that his films exploded the bounds of everyday humdrum Hollywood reality. His work previous to *The Fisher King* insured that. Even though our story was set in a somewhat controlled milieu, Terry encouraged all of us to stretch and expand our limits as Richard had done with the script. He was literally our leader in reaching for the stars as well as the Holy Grail.

I remember so clearly the morning I showed Terry the work which represented Parry's homage and obsession with the Red Knight. I think our director liked what he saw, but he drove me on to elaborate on what I had done and what we had talked about. It was as if he set me free, and now was the time for uninhibited creative activity to make a visual that would be an exciting depiction of that Red Knight. The result for me was an exhilarating satisfaction. With Terry the hard work was appropriate, imaginative, exciting and FUN!

BILL CRUSE,

Even at our first meeting, Terry was at once disarmingly friendly and subtly intimidating. His reputation as a *visual* perfectionist with a razor sharp eye precedes him, yet his sense of humor and that slightly maniacal grin put us strangely at ease. We were not just working on another movie, rather we had become Knights of Terry's slightly ovoid Round Table, urged on by his contagious enthusiasm for the quest; for the shot, for the film, and, perhaps, for the grail of *The Fisher King* itself.

GEORGE FENTON,

Charlotte Street, November 1990. I haven't seen Ray Cooper for 12 years when we met in this very street (different restaurant). He hasn't changed. I still wish I wore his clothes, drove his car, smoked his cigars. Apart from his talent, I always feel he should be included on the Civil List just for spreading good taste. He's introducing me to Terry Gilliam, whom although I've never met, is just as I remember him from what Lesley, Jeremy and Kevin have been telling me about him and *The Fisher King*. It all sounds bewildering and remains so during lunch. Terry is like the guy that's just invented the wheel.

He asks me to see the film. Discreet thumbs up from the cutting room — Thanks — maybe this is going to work out. The film is amazing: nothing could have prepared me for this and afterwards I mutter feeble generalizations, feeling so far behind the Gilliam roller coaster. We start to spot the picture and things become surprisingly clear. Terry knows about the music like he knows about the camera and the design and the cut and everything else and the new normality of *The Fisher King* enters my life. It's highly infectious. I fiddle about with themes, play them to Terry and Ray. Terry suggests things — I try them — this is great, I feel none of the usual loneliness associated with this part of the process. We invite Harry Nilsson over and he sings "How About You" with Ronnie Price playing the piano. Just the five of us and it's a perfect moment. We start recording in CTS. Debra's been around while I've been writing, but I'm still hoping for a good reaction from her and Lynda. They seem to like it. So does Terry, so does Keith, so do I and so it goes, The Waltz, The Walk to the Chinese Restaurant, The Nightmare, The Chase and, of course, "How About You."

Twice I've been to New York since we finished and as I lob out money to the homeless people on the street, I find I'm looking for Parry and although someone is playing the saxophone in Grand Central Station, how come no one's dancing? It wouldn't seem strange to me. Terry, what have you done?

KEITH GRECO & VINCENT JEFFERDS,

We're in training for medieval boot camp, preparing for an offensive in Central Park. Our Commander-in-Grief/Coxswain exhorts from shore, bellowing contradictory directions. But his breath is not in vain, for it carries the virus that will focus us, and as the infection progresses, every taco chip, rusted can and plate of pasta will reveal itself as yet another manifestation of the Red Knightmare. These symptoms verify his diagnosis. "Good, the Rot has set in." Our leader is insatiable: we can do no right, but must press on.

Occasionally we are allowed to rest, by mistake. We wake in mid-Manhattan clutching halberds and swords. "No, No, No, you've lost it, you've fallen in love with it again, you've got to fuck it up some more." And we did, because for everything Terry took, he gave us something back, which is refreshing when you're in a process that can never end. Time just runs out, period.

LYNDA OBST & DEBRA HILL,

Sitting in the offices of CAA, the central directorate of Hollywood directors, with five agents named Mike — none of them the famous one. Down the formidable list of formidable directors, some kind of abstract shopping list. The wrong choice here and we've sunk the best script we've ever had. We'll never forget this moment:

Mike No. 1 says, "What about Terry Gilliam!" The room is silent, as the truth and fearsomeness of the notion takes root. Terry Gilliam — visionary anarchist, torturer of studio heads, annihilator of producers, grand architect of the imagination. The Red Knight was meant to be drawn by him. With this thought, though without any inkling as to its likelihood in the practical world, *Fisher King*, which we had coddled, nourished and protected up till then — met its maker. And we met the dragon-slayer we would forever after slay dragons for.

LESLEY WALKER,

Working with Terry was the kind of experience that leaves you wondering why all films can't be like this. His generosity as a person and the natural way in which he gives credit to those around him can be best explained by one of my many experiences with him:

Throughout the shooting of the picture, Terry only saw a couple of scenes cut together. I had never worked with him before, so when the time came to show him my first cut (just over three hours in length) I was sick with nerves — what if I was on the wrong wavelength; what if he didn't like the way I edited; the list could go on and on.

Terry arrived for the screening — I'd last seen him on the final day of shooting, two weeks earlier, in L.A. — and immediately he spotted something was wrong: the wringing of hands, the pallid face, etc. , and he asked what was up. I replied that I was nervous and he asked why. I explained. He said, "Don't be nervous; if there is anything wrong with the film then *I've* fucked up." That sums up Terry's generosity. The running was still a nightmare for although I loved the film, there was three hours of agonizing over every cut.

The film ends. Lights up. Silence. Be brave. Turned to look at him. Then this huge Terry grin. He loved the movie. Of course, there was work to do — the whole of post-production was the most wonderful experience, like the filming — a great collaboration with Terry at the helm. I can't wait for the next time.

CREDITS

TRI-STAR PICTURES PRESENTS

A HILL/OBST PRODUCTION

A TERRY GILLIAM FILM

ROBIN WILLIAMS

JEFF BRIDGES

"THE FISHER KING"

AMANDA PLUMMER

and MERCEDES RUEHL

Casting by
HOWARD FEUER

Costume Designer
BEATRIX PASZTOR

Music by
GEORGE FENTON

Editor
LESLEY WALKER

Production Designer
MEL BOURNE

Director of Photography
ROGER PRATT, B.S.C.

Written by
RICHARD LaGRAVENESE

Produced by
DEBRA HILL and
LYNDA OBST

Directed by
TERRY GILLIAM

Also Starring
MICHAEL JETER
WILLIAM JAY MARSHALL
CHRIS HOWELL

CAST OF CHARACTERS
(In Order of Appearance)

Jack ....JEFF BRIDGES
Radio Engineers ....ADAM BRYANT
                                                                                                              PAUL LOMBARDI
Lou Rosen..DAVID PIERCE
Limo Bum .... TED ROSS
Sondra ....LARA HARRIS
TV Anchorman .... WARREN OLNEY
News Reporter...FRAZER SMITH
Anne...MERCEDES RUEHL
Crazed Video Customer.. KATHY NAJIMY
Sitcom Actor Ben Starr .... HARRY SHEARER
Sitcom Wife ....MELINDA CULEA
Bum at Hotel ....JAMES REMINI
Doorman..MARK BOWDEN
Father at Hotel ....JOHN OTTAVINO
Little Boy .... BRIAN MICHAELS
First Punk .... JAYCE BARTOK
Second Punk .... DAN FUTTERMAN
Parry..ROBIN WILLIAMS
Hippie Bum.. BRADLEY GREGG
Jamaican Bum ....WILLIAM JAY MARSHALL
John the Bum .... WILLIAM PRESTON
Superintendent ....AL FANN
Porno Customer .... STEPHEN BRIDGEWATER
Lydia .... AMANDA PLUMMER
Stockbroker Bum... JOHN HEFFERNAN
Red Knight .... CHRIS HOWELL
Homeless Cabaret Singer...MICHAEL JETER
Strait Jacket Yuppie...RICHARD LaGRAVENESE
Bag Lady... ANITA DANGLER
Drooler...MARK BRINGELSON
Pizza Boy ....JOHNNY PAGANELLI
Receptionist.. DIANE ROBIN
Motorcyclist .... JOHN BENJAMIN RED
Parry's Wife ....LISA BLADES
Edwin.. CHRISTIAN CLEMENSON
Doctor ....CARLOS CARRASCO
Guard .... JOE JAMROG
TV Executive...JOHN de LANCIE
Nurse.. LOU HANCOCK
Radio Show Call-Ins .... CAROLINE CROMELIN
                                                                                     KATHLEEN BRIDGET KELLY
                                                                                                         PATRICK FRALEY
Stunts ....JANET BRADY
                                                                                                          GREG BRICKMAN
                                                                                                          JOPHREY BROWN

188

Stunts, continued	LLOYD CATLETT
	GILBERT COMBS
	PETE CORBY
	JEFF DASHNAW
	ANDY DUPPIN
	J.B. GETZWILLER
	BONNIE HOCK
	RIKKE KESTEN
	HARRY MADSEN
	BENNIE MOORE
	JULIE STONE
Associate Producer	STACEY SHER
Unit Production Manager/Associate Producer	ANTHONY MARK
First Assistant Directors	DAVID McGIFFERT
	JOE NAPOLITANO
Second Assistant Director	CARLA CORWIN
Second Second Assistant Director	CYNTHIA A. POTTHAST
Script Supervisor	MARION TUMEN
Art Director	P. MICHAEL JOHNSTON
Set Decorator	CINDY CARR
Art Department Assistant	ANNE HARMON
Set Designers	JASON R. WEIL
	RICK HEINRICHS
Model Consultants	BILL CRUSE & CO.
Leadmen	DAVID C. POTTER
	KRISTEN KELLY
Property Master	LARRY CLARK BIRD
Assistant Property Masters	KEN ZIMMERMAN
	DAVID AARON
Camera Operator	CRAIG HAAGENSEN
First Assistant Camera	NICHOLAS J. MASURACA
Second Assistant Camera	GREGORY D. WALTERS
	CHUCK WHELAN
Assistant Film Editor	JEREMY HUME
Assistant Film Editors USA	EDWARD STABILE
	TARA TIMPONE
Second Assistant Film Editor	TULLIO BRUNT
Apprentice Film Editor USA	TRISTAN BRIGHTY
Sound Editor	PETER PENNELL
Assistant Sound Editor	STEFNA BORGES
Dialogue Editor	ALAN PALEY
Assistant Dialogue Editor	ANDREW MELHUISH
Foley Editor	BOB RISK
Assistant Foley Editor	STEVE MAGUIRE
Music Editor	KEVIN LANE
Music Consultant	RAY COOPER
Sound Mixer	THOMAS CAUSEY

Boom Operators ....JOSEPH F. BRENNAN
RICHARD KITE
Re-Recording Mixers .... PAUL CARR
ROBERT FARR
Video Assist Operator ....NEIL S. BUCKHANTZ
Post-Production Supervisor ....SHARRE JACOBY
Chief Lighting Technician.. JAMES PLANNETTE
Lighting Technicians ....R. MICHAEL DECHELLIS
JOHN GUTIERREZ
Rigging Gaffer ....ANDY NELSON
Electrical Best Boy .... PAUL ARY
Best Boy .... ROGER BLAUVELT
Key Grip .... MARTY EICHMANN
Second Grip...STEPHEN V. ISBELL
Dolly Grip ....ANTONIO V. GARRIDO
Grips.. PATRICK SHAUN BARD
WILLIAM R. TAYLOR
PAUL DAVID WILLIAMS
Creative Special Effects Consultant..ROBERT E. McCARTHY
Special Effects Supervisor...DENNIS DION
Special Effects ....DAN SUDICK
Costume Supervisor ....JOIE HUTCHINSON
Costumer.. LINDA LOUISE TAYLOR
Assistant to Costume Supervisor..RANDY STARCK
Red Knight Costume Designed by ....KEITH GRECO
VINCENT JEFFERDS
Wardrobe Research Assistant .... RAINER JUDD
Key Make-Up Artist... ZOLTAN ELEK
Key Hairstylist... LISA JOY MEYERS
Stunt Coordinator .... CHRIS HOWELL
Choreographer .... ROBIN HORNESS
Location Manager .... BILL BOWLING
Assistant Location Manager..JAMES R. MACEO
Special Projects .... BARRY ROSENBUSH
Publicity...SUSAN PILE
Still Photographers .... JOHN CLIFFORD
STEPHEN VAUGHAN
Transportation Coordinator ....EDWARD F. VOELKER
Transportation Captain...JAMES W. ROBERTS
Construction Coordinator..RICHARD DEAN RANKIN
Construction Foreman... DAVID B. BRENNER
Labor Foreman ....MANUEL SILVIA
Paint Foreman..MAURICE E. LARSON
GIOVANNI FERRARA
Propmaker Foreman...DALE GORDON
Musco Light Technician .... RON KUNECKE
Production Coordinator...PAM CORNFELD
Production Secretary .... SHARYN SHIMADA

uction Accountant .... MARGARET A. MITCHELL
ssistant Accountants .... VERONICA CLAYPOOL
GARY McCARTHY, JR.
Assistant to Debra Hill .... VALENCIA GIACCO
Assistant to Lynda Obst .... CARMEN B. WEETS
Assistant to Terry Gilliam .... YVETTE S. TAYLOR
Assistant to Anthony Mark .... ANN WEISS-LaGRAVENESE
Casting Assistant .... ALISHAN COKER
Production Assistants .... MARK GALLEY
TR JONES
TRAVIS KEYES
BARBARA LAMPSON
AMY LOVE
NICOLE MILLER
ELLIE SMITH
MICHAEL VIGLIETTA
DGA Trainee .... MARGARET PIANE
DJ Consultant .... STEPHEN BRIDGEWATER
News Report Supervisor .... NANCY PLATT JACOBY
Horses Owned and Trained by .... JAMES ZOPPE
Animal Colorist .... DOUGLAS J. WHITE
Artwork Donated by .... SY and JESSICA SHER
Post-Production Facilities .... PROMINENT STUDIOS
Re-recorded at .... ROGER CHERRILL'S
Titles by .... CHRIS ALLIES
Opticals and Visual Effects by .... PEERLESS CAMERA COMPANY LTD.

NEW YORK UNIT
Assistant Unit Production Manager/Location Manager .... MARK A. BAKER
Set Decorators .... KEVIN McCARTHY
JOSEPH L. BIRD
Chargeman Scenic Artist .... MICHAEL ZANSKY
Property Master .... TOM WRIGHT
Assistant Property Master .... THOMAS A. McDERMOTT
First Assistant Camera .... JONATHAN T. ERCOLE
Second Assistant Camera .... JOHN CAMBRIA
Sound Mixer .... DENNIS MAITLAND, II
Boom Operator .... JOHN K. FUNDUS
Cableman .... STEPHEN SCANLON
Video Assist Operator .... RICHARD MADER, JR.
Chief Lighting Technician .... KENNETH R. CONNORS
Rigging Gaffer .... ROBERT G. CONNORS
Key Grip .... MICHAEL MILLER
Second Grip .... THOMAS J. JIRGAL
Grips .... JIMMY FINNERTY, JR.
ROBERT MILLER
Special Effects Supervisor .... EDWARD DROHAN
Costumer .... MARY COLEMAN-GIERCZAK

Make-up Artist .... CRAIG LYN

Additional Location Manager .... MARK L. RHOL

Assistant Location Managers .... ANN F. MARKE

LAWRENCE P. GANEM

Assistant Production Accountants .... DESIREE PERRI

MARK J. LEVENSTEIN

Extras Casting .... TODD THALER

Transportation Captain .... JOHN LEONIDAS

Construction Coordinator .... ED FERRARO

Second Second Assistant Director .... CYD ADAMS

DGA Trainee .... REBECCA SAIONZ

Production Office Coordinator .... JACKIE MARTIN

Production Secretary .... JEANNE CHRZANOWSKI

Production Assistants .... TRISTAN BOURNE

PIERRE CAILLIAREC

TODD M. CAMNH

PATRICK D. GARRISON

MAUREEN GARVEY

KATHLEEN KELLY

TIMOTHY C. LEE

JASON MARK

CARRIE RUDOLF

JOHN RYBACKI

SPECIAL THANKS TO:

The Arthur Company
Caballero Home Video
Major Soccer League
Members Only
Metropolitan Transportation Authority
New York Post
Radio & Records
KFI Radio
KQLZ Pirate Radio

Billboard Magazine appears courtesy of
BPI Communications, Inc.

Tape material from "JEOPARDY!"
Courtesy of Jeopardy Productions, Inc.

Original Soundtrack Album Available on
MCA Records, Cassettes and Compact Discs

Additional Orchestrations ....JEFF ATMAJIAN
Synth Programming .... ADRIAN THOMAS
Music Scoring Mixers .... KEITH GRANT
SIMON SMART
GERRY O'RIORDEN
Music Recorded at ....C.T.S. STUDIO, LONDON, ENGLAND

"How About You"
Written by Ralph Freed & Burton Lane
Produced by Ray Cooper and George Fenton
Sung and Whistled by Harry Nilsson

"Chill Out Jack"
Written by Cave Samrai, Richard Williams,
Peter Harvey & Jonny Templeton
Performed by Trip
Courtesy of MCA Records

"Hit The Road Jack"
Written by Percy Mayfield
Performed by Ray Charles
Courtesy of Ray Charles Enterprises, Inc.

"I Wish I Knew"
Written by Harry Warren & Mack Gordon
Performed by Jack Coltrane
Courtesy of MCA Records

"I'm Sorry"
Written by Ronnie Self & Dub Allbritten
Performed by Brenda Lee
Courtesy of MCA Records

"Lydia The Tattooed Lady"
Written by E.Y. Harburg & Harold Arlen

"The Power"
Written by Benito Benitez, John Garrett III,
Toni C., Robert Frazier & Mark James
Performed by Chill Rob G
Remixed by Kevin Lane
Courtesy of Wild Pitch Records, Ltd.

"Rose's Turn"
Written by Stephen Sondheim & Jule Styne

"Some People"
Written by Stephen Sondheim & Jule Styne

"You're Having My Baby"
Written by Paul Anka

Color by TECHNICOLOR®

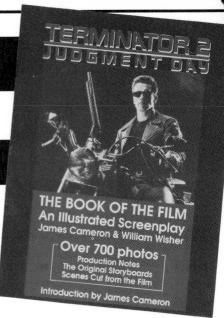